CLEOBURY MORTIMER

A SMALL MARKET TOWN BLIGHTED BY A DECADE OF POLITICAL CORRUPTION

BILLY C. MUMFORD

authorHOUSE®

AuthorHouse™ UK
1663 Liberty Drive
Bloomington, IN 47403 USA
www.authorhouse.co.uk
Phone: 0800.197.4150

Published by AuthorHouse   04/16/2015

ISBN: 978-1-5049-3692-7 (sc)
ISBN: 978-1-5049-3646-0 (hc)
ISBN: 978-1-5049-3693-4 (e)

Epigraph/Quotation on page 56 is from *The Gulag Archipelago* by Aleksandr
Solzhenitsyn, translated by Thomas P. Whitney. Published by The Harvill Press and
reproduced by permission of Editions Fayard and The Random House Group Ltd.

Print information available on the last page.

Any people depicted in stock imagery provided by Thinkstock are models,
and such images are being used for illustrative purposes only.
Certain stock imagery © Thinkstock.

This book is printed on acid-free paper.

CONTENTS

THANK YOU

To Ken Reynolds, John Griffiths, Martin Windridge, Julian Clelford and all those with well-meaning intentions who encountered deep flaws in Public Life, but they still valiantly maintained their fighting spirits.

ONE

Mumfords ironmongers shop

Mumfords has traded as an ironmongers store in Cleobury Mortimer for over 100 years with No. 2 Church Street being rather a handsome brick building situated in the centre of this small market town. It is a traditional business where nails are still sold by the pound, screws are sold singly, and shelves are crammed from floor to ceiling with useful everyday items like dolly pegs, moth balls, wax candles, enamel Billy cans, galvanised buckets, mutton cloth, laundry starch, tin baths, soap flakes, fork handles, enamel plates, fly killer papers, hurricane lamps, pure beeswax, tin mugs, carbolic soap, pick-axes – not an inch of space is wasted.

Most importantly Mumfords still continues to support its traditional values of respect, courtesy, honesty, trust, sincerity, integrity, kindness and service, just as it would have done a century ago. Our customers are also respectful of our traditions, hence we appreciate and value our customer base which provides us with a most pleasant working environment. We still embrace progress when we need to, but we have never allowed the modern world to compromise the values that form the very essence of what this business stands for.

Mumfords is superbly positioned, right in the middle of the High Street, across the road from the Church and the Market Hall; and in a curve in the road that gives a clear outlook both up and down the street. The central location of the shop enables us to be something of a focal point, a place where our customers come and chat about the 'ways of the world' and local issues, making this shop a hub for the exchange of local gossip.

Mumfords is fortunate that it has always traded well, and felt that its place was as part of a healthy trading community, but we have been saddened to see the demise of so many of our neighboring businesses which have closed at a rate of about 100 each decade. Despite so much in its favour our trading community was rapidly shrinking. The economy had taken a tumble, but Cleobury Mortimer has the advantage of location, being on a good tourist route which brings visitors to the town every day; however, it has been a combination of underlying factors that are to blame for economic decline.

Two grant-funded surveys conducted by the University of Worcester concluded that a significant percentage of the Cleobury hinterland which consisted of eight surrounding parishes, used Cleobury Mortimer often for basic purchases; but that apart, indications were still suggesting that all was not well in our community, scratch below the surface and nothing was quite as it seemed. One of the most obvious changes had been the lack of social cohesion and the increase in hostility, but it would take many years to discover that Cleobury Mortimer was entering a period of confusion and turbulence, and that we were in for a rough ride.

The first decade of the second millennium has seen an unprecedented change in society at large; the huge advancement in technology opening up a whole new world through communication and easy access to information. However, this progress has come simultaneously with a shift in the values that underpin our society. Who would have expected that we would reach an era when it is so difficult to trust anyone? This has been epitomised by the number of high profile public scandals that have engulfed every sector of society and public life; but worst of all is the loss of trust in one another as human beings.

Who would have expected policemen to behave like crooks? Who would have expected hospitable workers to be cruel to their patients? Who would have expected civil servants and Governance to be corrupt? Who would have expected the Church to cover-up so many cases of abuse? Who would have expected newspaper editors to be such propagandists? Who would have expected solicitors and lawyers to pervert the course of justice? Yet, in Nov. 2013 the Coroner for Gloucester, a solicitor, named Alan Crickmore was jailed for stealing £2million from his vulnerable clients to fund his lavish lifestyle! The matter only came to light through an audit in 2008, but for all crooks to succeed, they must have the knowledge that the likelihood of being caught is remote. Good gracious, can things get any worse!

Hunkydory If everything had been hunkydory in our town there would be no need to be writing this account, but that has not been so, and there is risk that historical references will contain no accurate account of the sequence of events that blighted this community from 1999 to 2014. This era has been so troubled by malpractice that even public records from our Parish Council meetings have been falsified and manipulated and cannot be relied upon for accuracy.

Just a small handful of people Cleobury Mortimer has a population of just over 3000, but for such a small town it has a range of social problems, but the worst aspect is the rather unpleasant culture that has taken a stranglehold, though it is possible to narrow this influence down to just a handful of people whose detrimental actions and influences have poisoned the minds of others to create a fractured community in a dark and generally ungoverned place.

Now don't be tempted to judge this account before you know the whole story As bad as the situation has at times been, there are still those of us familiar enough with public standing and public expectation to know that there is really no place in any civilised community for dodgy politics, dodgy politicians or dodgy public records. So another purpose of creating this account is to serve as a reminder to those who maybe thought that they could exploit political apathy and avoid accountability, that in fact the electorate still has a high level of expectation, and that this bench-mark must never be compromised.

Reflecting the golden era of times gone by Those of us who recall happier times, 1999 is a date that provides a significant bench mark. The decades before 1999 saw happier times in Cleobury Mortimer, it was a different era, but also a much more pleasant one; there was less opportunity for prosperity and times were leaner, but there was also less pressure and less expectation, and generally people got on together, there was tolerance and respect; people were more contented, more community minded, kinder. This was a friendly, vibrant and commercially prosperous market town both economically and socially, with shops and public houses stretching up the road towards Ludlow and down the road into Lower Street. An era with a strong community spirit, a time when the town took care of itself and those within it. We had natural leadership, which was a broad spectrum of good people from the local and the business community who cared about the town we lived and worked in; they gave their time and their skills to ensure that Cleobury Mortimer was as nice a place as it could possibly be.

Fond memories There are fond memories of Mr. Ralph Jones, Mrs. Gittens from The Lea Farm, Mr. Frank Pain, and Mr. Tom Pain; their presence gave reassurance, their passion and concern for the town and its residents was sincere. Mr. Tom Pain was one of the last of that generation, an entrepreneur and business man he was well-known and highly respected, and at one time he even owned the Mumfords retail premises. We recall that despite his advancing years Mr. Pain, a tall and distinguished gentleman, regularly walked around the town, always with a kindly word or cheery greeting for anyone he encountered. But Mr. Tom Pain was remembered for his community spirit, his generosity and his kindness, his helpfulness towards others in need within the community, and at Christmas he was known to dispatch hampers to those he knew would appreciate them. With the passing of these people the town became devoid of natural leadership, and a downward spiral began. It would be fair to say that for all the years until 1999 the Cleobury electorate had no need to concern itself with local politics, the town was in the safest of hands.

Vantage point At Mumfords we have an ideal vantage point, standing on the steps of our shop we have quietly observed many changes, some good, some not so good, and some bad. This account is to provide a reliable record of some of the issues that have had a deeply profound and fundamental impact on our community both economically and socially. Looking at the changes in our town there is a need to make the comparison with what we observe in society at large, where, let's face it, incredible advances in technology have transformed how we all live our lives. So our observations take into account the whole of society, and the way that world-wide influences beyond our control can still have a negative impact on our own rural way of life.

Troubled times Nothing stays the same forever, the unexpected is always just around the corner and all sorts of negative factors came from nowhere and began taking a stranglehold of Cleobury Mortimer plunging it at the edge of a moral cess-pit. We watched in stunned disbelief as the community spirit in our town slowly disintegrated as it became caught up in the cross-fire of political strife. We watched in frustration and despair as those in our town with working-class origins showed they had a better grasp of public moral values, as they valiantly challenged those who were abusing and trashing our local political system.

Since 1999 Cleobury Mortimer has become a troubled, and divided community; dominated by egotists, and political controversy so extreme that everyone is either in one camp or another. One has to ask, where on earth did these people come from? However, the stance has become so ingrained that it is unlikely to change until there is fresh impetus, a change in attitude, an uprising, or maybe the community might consider changing its apathetic approach and take more interest in public life if only to prevent the egotists and self-serving from having it all their own way.

Local influence Within any community leadership comes from institutions, in our case the Parish Council, and the Churches, so, it is in the interest of everyone that care is taken to ensure the very best leaders are elected; this is a crucial aspect of social responsibility. It becomes hugely beneficial when members of any community with appropriate credentials, leadership skills and genuine concerns for their town volunteer for public service.

TWO

Winston Churchill - 'Never yield to force, never to the apparently over-whelming might of the enemy'.

New Labour In the interests of transparency and to fully tell the story, the impact of New Labour needs to be put into perspective and to do that that we need to take a look nationally at what happened in 1995; this was when Labour re-branded its party in an attempt to widen its electoral appeal. New Labour was launched, and the party went on to win the general election in 1997 with a landslide victory. This result brought with it a new type of governance that we were later to learn was based on sleaze, manipulation and spin. The antics of the Labour leaders are now legendry, their influence became hugely detrimental to politics in general, with examples of dirty tricks giving credence for some politicians with questionable integrity to similarly use corrupt practice to suite any warped political agenda. Sadly, the days when politicians could be trusted have long gone.

The most devisive Parish Council in memory It soon became evident that the negative influences of New Labour in Westminster were spreading across the country and had reached South Shropshire. Following our local elections there has not been a more divisive Parish Council in Cleobury Mortimer in living memory, people who used to tolerate one another were forced to side one way or another. This newly elected Council considered it had a certain knowledge of superiority in what it regarded as best for the town, classing those who did not agree with them as inferior. Later on it would be their lying ways and their shallow, facile, sanctimonious, self-serving, failure to answer perfectly straightforward questions about an avalanche of allegations that became so confusing and frightening, that it lead to their downfall. For the first time we saw the introduction of propaganda and spin into Cleobury Mortimer's political agenda.

Good times were expected It is only as we reflect back that we notice these things, at the time no-one expected things could turn out as badly as they did. In fact we thought that the new Millennium would bring forth a new style of governance, these were changing and exciting times after all. Besides the newly elected Cleobury Council consisted of some teachers, and supposedly respected local people; collectively they offered opportunity for positive change, the chance to give the town fresh impetus. However, this new Council did not conduct itself in a manner that entirely befitted the position of trust and responsibility in which it was placed. Instead the results from the ballot box would emerge to become the start of the most disappointing and troubling era.

Firstly they installed a Class system. The new Parish Council members appointed at the end of the last millenium considered themselves so frightfully important they regarded themselves as Upper Class, the rest of us particularly, if we were in trade, were to know our place, we were working class! Whilst they basked in the euphoria of having a major project to focus on, it became evident that the group lacked the skills, expertise and patience to make wise and prudent decisions, particularly with the complex restoration of the Market Hall. They were so unwise to make the infamous comment 'We are awash with grant money'. Sadly, it all went terribly wrong for the Upper Class, for it all ended in tears; they were soon out of office with reputations in tatters. The legacy of the fallout from their dramatic fall from grace, plagues this town even today, through 'Bad Attitudes', and as we know, vengeance can be dangerous, it eats away and becomes a destructive force.

Bewdley by-pass An interesting theory suggested that pleasant times were remembered when this part of Shropshire was like a sleepy back-water, in a bygone age prior to 1987, and before the opening of the new Bewdley by-pass. The bye-pass opened up potential and opportunities, and triggered an increase in commuting. Houses were built and the town expanded, attracting people looking for cheaper accommodation, as house prices here are generally lower. An observation was made at the time that Cleobury Mortimer had become a haven for 'academics who had failed to reach potential in their working lives, and were seeking any sort of public office as a last ditch attempt at notoriety'. Whether there is any substance to this theory or not is questionable, but it is thought provoking, and goes some way to explain where the influence of 'Bad Attitude' came from when there was no evidence of it before.

'The Bad Attitude' This is a combination, of characteristics - egotism, arrogance, self-importance, and a dash of psychopathy thrown in. It is certainly contagious, and we have seen how it spreads, generally through like-minded people, who gravitate together, and now it has formed an underlying culture that blights this community to the extent that personalities and characters have been changed beyond recognition, and we see how hatred and jealousy is etched in the minds of the those who regularly occupy public seats, looking for trouble. There is need to find a collective name for a group of people with 'Bad Attitudes', any suggestions? The normal habitat for 'Bad Attitudes' is anywhere near public office, they like the chance to be prominent and assertive, then the effect becomes similar to that of falling in with a 'bad crowd'. Having infiltrated Cleobury Mortimer politics since 1999, it was a shock to discover cases of 'Bad Attitudes' emerging in Neen Savage during 2012.

The Storm clouds were gathering Even at the end of 2014, each monthly meeting of Neen Savage Parish Council finds the public seats filled with, yes . . . 'Bad Attitudes'. A characteristic of a 'Bad Attitude' is that they seem to have rather a lot of time on their hands, and it is most likely that their lives could be infinitely dull, as they seem to consider it rather sporting to sit for several hours observing public meetings where the dialogue can be very tedious; and where maybe there is little on the agenda to arouse much excitement; but they can still manage to be aroused to grumble and mumble, and hiss and spit, all the time with sour facial expressions. Any progress of the new Neen Savage Council has been hampered by this dominant culture that has been determined by aggressive and loud-mouthed people.

Cleobury Mortimer Public Interest Audit Report In September 2005 we read the Public Interest Audit Report 2003 produced by UHY Hacker Young, and the Audit Commission, who had been appointed jointly to audit the accounts of Cleobury Mortimer Parish Council for 2002, following the disastrous financial crisis incurred by the Council 1999-2003 as it restored the Market Hall. It was a damning report that concluded that 'Overall the project was characterised by weaknesses in corporate governance, project management and project control. The financial consequences of the additional expenditure had seen severe. It was recognised that the Council was unlikely to undertake a project on that scale in the near future, nevertheless there were important lessons to be learned'. In fact this was the second report to be published, the first report was particularly damning and the Councillors involved threatened the Auditors with legal action for defamation of character! So, a second Audit Report was produced that was toned down.

Here we go again - 2012 A decade after that report was issued it became apparent that no lessons had been learned; and a different controlling group was making similarly reckless decisions. So in dismay we observed all over again a new Cleobury Parish Council of 2012 nose-diving into yet another financial fiasco, through corrupt practice and ineptitude; as the Muller land project was trundled through. Curiously, there has been no close scrutiny of the questionable procedures behind this dodgy deal, so they will get a brief mention here.

Need for the National press Posters displayed on Mumfords shop window early in 2014 commenting on all the incidents of local political malpractice, so infuriated a local political figure that police were instructed to intervene; and with a certain irony this provided a conclusion from a police legal representative that in fact the problems blighting Cleobury Mortimer politics should really be in the National press!!

Shafted From the vantage point of our shop steps we have observed as the electorate has been shafted so many times. The electorate in Cleobury Mortimer and also in Neen Savage is entitled to feel like a bunch of mugs, because make no mistake, they have been mugged.

Democracy We believe in democracy, just as we believe in community spirit, fairness, kindness, respect, tolerance, trust and opportunity. We always assumed that those elected to represent us in Governance be it locally or national do so with the best of intentions and always with the utmost integrity. There is usually no reason to be suspicious of those who represent us, but we are living in very different and devious times.

So why did it all go wrong? Local politics consists of different tiers of leadership, at local and county level. A county Unitary Council has been operative since 2007 when Shropshire County elected to support Unitary status. Weakness in implementing disciplinary guidelines and levels of public expectation has much to answer for.

Code of conduct 2007 The electorate is reassured that Shropshire Council has a Code of Conduct in place that ensures that all those in public office adhere to a required level of expectation. The Code of Conduct comprises of the following General Principles: – Selflessness; Integrity; Objectively; Accountability; Openness; Honesty; Leadership.

However, two factors relating to the Code of Conduct need to be brought to public attention:

- **Firstly** – Local councillors habitually abuse their positions and ignore the expectation of the Code of Conduct.
- **Secondly** – Shropshire Council Legal and Democratic Services are exceptionally lax in implementing the Code of Conduct, and has demonstrated a tendency to initiate a cover-up rather than ensure that any errant public figure is reprimanded or brought to account when complaints are made.

However, in recent years it has been necessary to report public figures for breach of Code of Conduct in both Cleobury Mortimer and Neen Savage, many times, but any complaints to the county's administrative regulatory body have been dismissed, leading to question if the service is fit for purpose, with the practice of holding hearings behind closed doors, a policy that only fuels a cover-up culture if ever there was one. The purpose of the county's regulatory body is surely to protect the interests of the public, not to provide a cover-up facility for unscrupulous public figures. If the issues had been treated with the seriousness they merited and robust enquires were held, it would have curbed the culture of mal-practice, and public confidence would have been retained. All public figures are always elected in good faith, so it is with enormous disappointment that once in office they can sometimes lack the integrity that the position requires, with the temptation to betray the electorate, abuse their positions and reflect the shabby political culture so prevalent in the politics of today. The trouble usually begins when they start to believe their own hype, then their feet soon leave the ground as they follow their big heads skywards.

Suspended Over a decade ago a prominent local public figure was suspended from office for three months for breaching the County Councils Code of Conduct; but that was during a different era, well before the lax discipline stance kicked in. Does it appear that no lessons were learned from that experience, as that person's conduct remains just as corrupt in 2014? Whilst any well-meaning intensions were not in doubt, some errant public figures have continued to sit in meetings stoking up tensions, reflecting that this is all too often a dirty political game being played out. It is also demonstrated that all too often the politics of public figures are based on crude populist appeal to the powerless, and their behavior can be symptomatic of a far deeper malaise which must never be deemed acceptable, distorting the truth to ensure that views exist on borrowed detail, confirming that far too many public servants will always abuse power.

How brazen At the official count following the County elections of 2013, one of our public figures had the audacity to publicly claim that his successful campaign and re-election established that he was exonerated from all allegations that had been made against him. What absolute nonsense, the election result established that social media had been successfully exploited to shaft the Cleobury Mortimer electorate, yet again. Typifying how modern day influences have turned local politics into a dangerous game.

Hypocrisy Local public figures have breached many of the principles of the Code of Conduct during their time in office. When it comes to hypocrisy some public figures appear to be in a class of their own, using a cocktail of charm and contempt in an attempt to turbo charge their political careers. Surrounding themselves with a coterie of powerful political pals to bolster their images; they are most comfortable dispensing questionable wisdom at public meetings, where they operates through a deception that contaminates local politics, just like bad apples contaminate a fruit bowl, preying on confusion to create the most shocking and lethal consequences. They have the ability to tell political 'porkies' with remarkably telling ease, and flaunt their deception with pride, targeting young and impressionable people through social media; the most disturbing aspect is that far too many of them probably believe their own hype.

Do some Councillors consider it pay-back time? It is quite baffling why some Councillors have emerged to become such disappointing public figures, particularly when they have a natural ability for such a position; but once settled in office the lack of integrity soon sorts the wheat from the chaff; and those who possess appropriate credentials and those who don't. The conduct of one publicly elected official raised the question whether their negative conduct in public office suggested an act of vengeance against the community. Prior to public office this official had endured a certain amount of alienation from the community for many years; it was during an era when folk were not so broad-minded or tolerant, but no, despite protestation from supporters like ourselves, the community had not been particularly tolerant.

Charlatans Before they became errant some of our public figures had always been favored with a generous amount of reasonable doubt, and we at Mumfords feel particularly let down, as we had clearly misjudged the motives of many of these people. We had encouraged and supported them into public office, with our claim that 'Vote for these candidates, they are young, dynamic and will make such a difference to our Council', we just did not expect it to be a negative difference, and that their objectives would always smack of self-promotion. So through their subsequent fall from grace, we feel we have been duped by a bunch of Charlatans.

A dodgy planning job A local public figure became engrossed in a dodgy planning job in our town, where planning permission had been granted on a building at the rear of a property owned by the public figure. However, when the building work was underway, several aspects of the application were deliberately in breach of planning and listed building consent to the extent that it became detrimental to the adjoining property. The builders were aware that the work they were doing was in breach of the planning approval, but they were told to ignore the problem and carry on. The public figure was irritated that the neighbour affected should persist with complaints about the deliberate breaches, so a campaign of harassment began, where false and malicious public comments were made through the Council that had serious and defamatory intent against the innocent neighbour; giving the public the impression that police had intervened, when nothing of the sort had happened. The public official was abusing position in a manner that was intended to frighten the neighbour into 'backing-off' and being silent. Visions of a political thug come straight to mind.

Compromising position The use of intimidation against anyone who complained or made a negative comment was a ploy to distract from the compromising positions this public figure often found himself to be in. At a Parish Council meeting during spring of 2012, a journalist was present, and the face of the errant public figure became etched with embarrassment that the risk of being caught out again could be imminent; with an application for work that had already been completed, now before the Council! The application was posted with the name of the applicant erased, with the hope that the public would not notice, and neither would the journalist. The application received scant mention before swiftly moving onto the next agenda item. The following month the application was rejected. With so much serious malpractice conducted during his time in public life, it should have been time for the public figure to revert to that old fashioned virtue – resignation.

THREE

'Honesty in politics is just like oxygen, the
higher you get the less there is of it.'

A **need to shape up** The Tory Government at Westminster had failed
to gain a majority at the last general election in 2010, and since then has
struggled with a coalition Government with the Lib/Dems; coupled with
this has been the disturbing results continuously looming from opinion
polls that the odds could be stacked against the Tories winning at the
next general election in 2015. However, in Shropshire the Tory party has
a healthy majority holding about forty-seven of the seventy-four seats on
Shropshire Council; so it might have been expected that with this strong
position, there was no need for the temptation to trash both Council values
and Tory values. So, come on leadership it's time to shape-up.

'All power corrupts, but absolute power corrupts absolutely'.

The problem of public apathy Public apathy is a serious problem in
Shropshire, and much was done prior to the last election to arouse political
interest, but to no avail; there was a turn-out of only about 33% which
meant that two-thirds of the electorate did not bother to vote. So statistics
become unreliable and mean that a political position could easily become
precarious. Despite its current strong position Shropshire Council had been
under Lib/Dem control for many years; probably due to its close proximity
to the Welsh border. So does this explain why the priority of Shropshire
Council appears to be ensuring it retains strong Tory control, hence the
need to protect the questionable reputations of any Tory supporting public
figures so valiantly? Shropshire Council has already experienced the loss
of a Tory seat in 2014 when a bi-election in Ludlow produced a successful
Lib/Dem in candidate Andy Boddington.

Has there been an unhealthy culture of control at the helm of Shropshire Council? A senior member of the County Council has the benefit of having his wife as a Council colleague, and their son married the daughter of a couple, who both held seats, on the County Council. Then it transpired, rather conveniently that the bridegroom is employed at Tory central office. Does this create an unhealthy environment for transparency and accountability, and does this not fuel greater likelihood of cover-up and collusion? This comment is only made because attempts to have public figures for our region brought to account for their breach of code of conduct have always been rejected, which suggests to us a possible 'cover-up culture' to protect Tory support.

What is the stance of Shropshire Council on malpractice? In this era of transparency and accountability, the question must be raised, why is there so much secrecy with Shropshire Council, and why is there need for a cover-up culture? Why do news reports not appear unless they have been approved by the County Council first? Why did a highly paid senior executive resign so mysteriously and at such short notice? Why did the Council refuse the Liberal and Labour calls for an investigation into this swift departure? What connection does the County Council have with the tragic victim of a paedophile case? Is Shropshire Council covering up for paedophilia within the Establishment, north of the border?

Shropshire Council Chief Executive The very swift resignation of the senior executive in 2012 throws up more questions than answers, and a probe has never been permitted, why not? The issues involving the paedophile victim appear to paint a rather murky picture of a group of public service departments. The victim was apparently a vulnerable young person who was exploited by a high profile Scottish paedophile ring, and it is claimed that she received payment in settlement of the abuse. There are further unpleasant issues in this complex case which involved the murder of a whistle-blower and the imprisonment of another. It is claimed that the victim and her Mother moved to Shropshire for their well-being, so why did Shropshire Council, Shropshire NHS and West Mercia Police become involved in a messy cover-up? Was Shropshire Council involved in the engineered proceedings of intimidation and harassment against the victim and her Mother?

So 'raising awareness' must become a new mantra While we are on the subject is it not time for serious questions to be asked as to why Shropshire Council is in such a serious financial predicament, and during these austere times how can a salary of £180,000 for a chief executive really be justified? With County Councils under less scrutiny is it left to the electorate to ensure money is well-spent? Incidentally 'How Councils waste your money' was a most interesting documentary by C4 dispatches

State self-regulation This must be the daftest means of regulation, and the easiest thing to exploit. Corrupt political practice involving many public figures has repeatedly been reported to Shropshire Council, but their policy of self-regulation was never likely to be effective. Following any complaint The Legal and Democratic Services writes to the accused public figure and asks them if they have 'been naughty'. They say no they haven't. End of enquiry. There is never an investigation, hence the facility for a cover-up policy. This response is symptomatic of a culture in which we are increasingly loosing trust; we are so often outraged by countless examples of ineptitude and rank dishonesty. We are also losing faith in other institutions we rely on for our security and well-being, with our confidence further dented by the inability of police to always tell the truth.

Need to send a message to society Essentially in South Shropshire we have in office some public figures who are at times less than honourable and just because they are often Tory supporting public figures does not mean it is OK. Failure to take responsibility wrecks public confidence. When you are not seriously challenged in any meaningful way, of course you get complacent and comfortable. County Council and Parish Council can amount to one giant conspiracy against the electorate. Surely there must be a mechanism in place to get rid of those who are corrupt, or is the Tory position so fragile that a cover-up policy is the only way to secure the next election.

Getting too close to home There was a time that whenever we heard of corruption, unpleasant incidents or adverse criminal activity, we did not have to concern ourselves too much, and neither did we need to engage with the details in any way; because the issues and incidents were always far off, and often associated with inner city depravation or gang-land war-fare. But society has changed bringing this negative culture closer to home, which is why we need to see our local political establishment responding in an appropriate way; using closer scrutiny to protect and uphold values, particularly if they are Tory values.

More and more cases of state corruption and collaboration are emerging, every week brings some horrific new story. Paedophile crimes have been covered up throughput the land, with shocking cases coming to light in Rochdale, Rotherham, Dyfed, Powys, Oxford, and all of them involve negligent Council response, coupled with the culture of ensuring the Council's reputation takes precedence. In each case it appears that powerful and influential figures are being allowed to behave outside the law with impunity, and this includes those who collaborate with them.

Yet the gallant efforts of courageous whistle-blowers who dare complain about such wrong-doings, usually result in brutal persecution by the state. These brave individuals become targeted by the authorities for attempting public exposure of any state malpractice. This is the position of our country today and it cannot be tolerated. We are faced with the moral cowardice of those who put their careers, promotional prospects and pensions first; but the electorate expects everything to be done within the correct framework, without exception, and those that seek to order and regulate our lives must always tell the truth.

Wise judgment An indication of the problems faced by society today has even been raised by the Pope who recently made powerful comments about how British society had been deeply affected by moral decline, and he urged the Government to restore moral guidelines. (It is not thought that the Pope excluded Shropshire Council from this directive).

Raising awareness helps We read that Rotherham Council in South Yorkshire is the first to come to mind when we think of putrid scandal perpetuated by a broken system. Abuse on a huge scale was carried out against vulnerable youngsters while Council services and police turned a blind eye to what was going on, both ignoring cries for help from victims; instead they each blamed systemic failures, but agreed that Council services offered a poor response by not doing enough. However, despite this being another case of an industrial level of dishonesty where police failed to serve the public without fear or favour, with honesty and integrity, it has been further agreed since, that simply by raising awareness the situation has been helped.

Establishment cover-up During December 2014 Dame Butler-Sloss said that evidence suggests there had been widespread Establishment cover-up of abuse, and confirmed that senior members of British society considered it far more important to protect members of the elite and politicians; compared with responding to complaints from victims which were less important, she added, that she agreed it was disgraceful and there was a need to cut the whole scandal apart. Details have emerged of a paedophile mafia that suppressed any attempt at exposing the culture within the high-end of society, including an incident in 1984 when twelve police officers were involved in obstructing a publication in Rochdale, when an attempt was made to expose details of sixteen MP's at the heart of the establishment who were involved in paedophile abuse.

Who guards the guards themselves? This was a question asked by Jacob Rees-Mogg in the Telegraph on 25/6/13. Answer - It can only be the people. This article was in response to disclosure that police officers had used an under-cover smear campaign to discredit the family of murdered teenager Stephen Laurence. It was the courage of whistleblowers that revealed this shocking practice; so it is against this background that we, the public at large must act decisively to raise the expectations of the police force.

FOUR

Winston Churchill 1943 – 'How much easier it is to join bad company than to shake them off'.

Collision of legacies The troubles currently faced by Cleobury Mortimer come from a combination of factors that covered many years, but the fall-out has come from a collision of legacies. The first indication that Mumfords noticed that all was not as it should be, and that it was likely trouble was simmering, came from the Chamber of Trade. It was curious that a body that had such a crucial economic roll locally, was monopolised by a group of people who had no connection to trade at all. Those involved in this controlling group did not employ anyone and did not pay commercial rates, and they included, a jobbing gardener, a jornalist and a B&Q trolley collector; but somehow they were able to control the Chamber of Trade by apparently meeting some questionable criteria.

The Chamber of Trade Sadly the chamber no longer exists, but it had been established many years earlier to serve the local trading community and a constitution provided guidelines that defined the purpose of the chamber; that it should provide good will and support to its members without reservation. In 1998 the Chairman was Graham Brown who had a computer technology business, he had a shared objective to help promote his business and do the same for other chamber businesses. Always pleasant and friendly it was a shame when Graham was replaced as Chairman by a journalist who effectively knew nothing about the issues faced by the trading community.

That's no way for a Chairman to behave! What followed was a disturbing letter that Graham sent to the Chamber some months later. Five people were sat in a meeting in an oak lined room in Church Street, when the letter from Graham was read out 'Despite me being the immediate past Chairman I appear to be alienated from the Chamber, I receive no contact from anyone and I am never informed about meetings, can you please advise why?' The letter was passed to a Chairman, who simply tossed it aside, leaving the content never discussed, and neither was the courtesy of a response offered.

This incident would be the first occasion that demonstrated the contemptible style used by a group of egotistical people who set about systematically securing a stranglehold of this town that would last over a decade, and engulf the whole community. It became clear that despite the Chamber having a constitution, the constitution was never adhered to, the Chamber was not promoting local business, and neither did it ever cultivate trading friendships.

Superb location Cleobury Mortimer is situated in a superb location surrounded by a special landscape and beautiful views, much appreciated by walkers. Focal point in the town is the imposing St. Mary's Church with its notorious crooked steeple which entitled its membership of 'The twisted spires in Europe'. Our Church still has a fundamental roll with Christianity underpinning our national values, as we identify with our core values based on equality, compassion and understanding. St. Mary's provides a most attractive impact in our town which is basically a single main street on a good through route on the A4117 which carries lots of passing traffic, a road often regarded as the gateway to Shropshire. Adjacent to the Church stands The Market Hall a substantial stone built two-storey building, it is an imposing building, however, it became structurally unsafe during the nineties and remained boarded up for several years. It is a focal point that became something of an eye-sore, so the community welcomed any initiative to restore it. By 2001, apart from the Parish Council, St. Mary's Church was also contemplating taking on the restoration of the building for use as Church hall and for Sunday school use. This would have been the option that the town would have preferred, particularly as the building lent itself so well to the Church. Under the guidance of Mr. Jim Drennan the process of contemplating the viability of the project was underway, however, his efforts would soon be curtailed.

Unfortunate irony was about to raise its ugly head Besides being a public figure, one person happened to be influential on Chamber of Trade, and in that capacity he initiated an emergency meeting of the group, and using information that was only privy to public figures, in an attempt to manipulate proceedings. That same evening, several trading members were seated around a round table just inside the door of the Kings Arms pub. During that meeting there was just one item on the agenda:

1. To secure the agreement of the Cleobury trading community to support an initiative by the town's administration to convert the Market Hall into partial commercial premises, and partial function/meeting rooms.

Shock, horror! Some of us were quietly aghast, this was a rotten dirty trick, it was betrayal and an act of vindictiveness, and did not support the motion. Next morning we went to Rev. Robert Horsfield and relayed to him the events of the trading meeting the evening before. The Vicar responded that he could see what was happening – he said that the wife of the public figure in question had failed in a final attempt at promotion, and the Vicar said that he had been on the selection panel that made that decision. The Vicar said that we were witnessing revenge, with the public figure resorting to taking out vengeance on the community for that decision!

The unexpected is often just around the corner This was provided by the Foot and Mouth Disease outbreak in Feb. 2001 which came from no-where, and brought much of the country to a standstill. This contagious disease would have dire consequences for Agriculture and Tourism, costing the country £8.5 billion, affecting 2000 farms and 10 million animals were slaughtered. Cleobury Mortimer was not unduly affected, yet was not immune to the devastating consequences. The crisis must have had similar fall-out to that experienced during times of war, confusion was abound, and corruption became rife.

The crisis became a national power struggle, so shrouded in misinformation that it was only during the aftermath that it became possible to reconstruct what really happened. Farmers were wildly misled by all the propaganda from Government and from farming organisations, which raised the most serious political questions. A cull program was introduced in which millions of healthy animals were to die, but it would later be established that this policy of killing everything that may have had contact was actually in breach of EU and UK law. In over 100 cases where

Government officials were challenged, they had to back down and relent. But the vast majority of farmers clearly found it hard to believe that the Government might be in flagrant breach of the law, and most accepted the legality of the actions without challenge. They were further tempted to agree to the scheme by generous compensation.

Controlling the disease Practical science had to work within a framework of politics and morbid psychology; this then reinforced the already existing prejudice against vaccination, which emerged in the NFU v. Agricultural Ministry battle. So riddled did the vaccine battle become that genuine experts could only look on in disbelief. It was particularly telling that experienced and scientifically knowledgeable people were ignored and side-lined by the political New Labour establishment; who were preferring to base every argument without enough scientific fact; and during the fog of the time, the authority behind the argument became totally lost. The crisis was outplayed by what became a political game with grotesque blunders and amazing official arrogance that led to barbaric cruelty abounding.

Political mafia Government officials were accused of acting like the Mafia, and Phoenix the calf became a symbol that if you cannot change reality, then at least you can change the way it looks. Phoenix was a snowy white calf only a day old when somehow she managed to avoid the slaughter-men, who had killed the rest of her herd. A few day later, just as the slaughter-men were returning to finish the task, the story of Phoenix hit the headlines, and melted the hearts of the nation. It was fortuitous timing, an election year, Tony Blair was Prime Minister, and he had to take a tough decision as he had been quietly warned that slaying the calf would slam their election chances, particularly as The Sun produced a satirical front page: "Vote Labour, or the calf gets it!" The Government changed the slaughter policy and Phoenix was reprieved. (Happy note-Phoenix has just produced her fourth calf).

Grunty the pig This was another pet that was reprieved and gained notoriety, thanks to the decision of a High Court London Judge who, after a very costly legal battle considered it unlawful that Grunty should be killed under the Governments questionable slaughter policy. Up until then pets had been slaughtered without compassion

Suspicions behind the Foot and Mouth outbreak During the aftermath of the crisis, shocking claims emerged. A curious little riddle behind one story questioned why a team of epidemiologists from Imperial College London should out of the blue produce a report of previous epidemics of a disease which had not affected Britain for 30 years; this report was out of the research team's normal remit. But when Foot and Mouth disease appeared four months later it raised the question, was this a coincidence or did the team get word that a Foot and Mouth crisis was on the way. There are around seven strains of Foot and Mouth disease worldwide and it would emerge that the particular strain of virus involved in the 2001 outbreak could be traced to the Porton Down facility in Wiltshire in what was likely a deliberate act of bio-terrorism directed at farmers – who were at the time the biggest power block opposing the New Labour Government. The harsh reality of the prospect that this contagious disease may have been deliberately released by the Labour Government to bring the whole of the farming community to its knees is too horrendous a prospect to contemplate. Porton Down is one of the most sensitive and secretive experimental sites in the UK; it is also a world leader in high-quality microbiological research, protected by the highest security measures.

Adding further to the suspicions about the outbreak, it was claimed that three months before the first outbreak Government officials had contacted timber suppliers across the country, asking about the provision of timber sleepers for pyres; approaches were also made to sign makers, enquiring about their ability to mass produce signage. This seemed that preparations were well under way, and suggested that the Government was aware that an outbreak was imminent. Adding even further to the mystery, in Jan 2001 the EU Commission ordered the immediate testing of Foot and Mouth vaccine, (when the last epidemic had been in back in 1967), by the following month the whole country would be in the grip of the disease!

The Chinese revolt followed It is claimed most likely that the Government had a hand in using the epidemic to bring the farming community to its knees, but naturally they were rather keen that blame should be directed elsewhere. So in a crude attempt to divert attention from their possible involvement in the epidemic, the Agriculture Ministry directed some blame on Chinese restaurants in the north of England. This triggered a revolt with thousands of Chinese converging on Chinatown, London to be addressed by the Minister who was forced to accept culpability, with compensation subsequently being paid to the Chinese community. This demonstration, and the result, showed the strength inherent in any group that sticks together to fight against anything fundamentally wrong.

Warning – The Brussels impact Implications behind the manner in which this disease was used as a political weapon should serve as a warning about questionable Government influence and the potential for, and risk of, coercion within society and with our own communities. When observers have looked more carefully at evidence behind spates of political interference, there was several reasons to question whether situations were truly as rosy as they are made to look. The Government's handling of the whole Foot and Mouth crisis seemed deeply flawed and at times inefficient; but it was not revealed until much later that in fact the power to respond to any Foot and Mouth crisis that should affect the UK, had been transferred to Brussels way back in 1980 through document 85/511. So despite the criticism directed at the Government, the ultimate control of the disease in our country was influenced by hidden European dimensions.

FIVE

Proverbs 28 v 6: - 'Better is a poor man who walks in his integrity than a man who is rich and perverse in his ways'.

Every cloud has a silver lining The aftermath of the Foot and Mouth crisis brought forth opportunities. In Cleobury Mortimer the Council of 1999 was already contemplating the renovation of the Market Hall, when news was received that the Government was making substantial grant aid available to help rejuvenate rural communities that had suffered from the loss of tourism trade, caused by movement restrictions imposed by the Foot and Mouth epidemic. Hence the development of the Market Hall project by the Parish Council was well timed with all the extra funding that was to become available. However, the Market Hall restoration would become a contentious saga with a fall-out that remains a shadowy presence even today. Firstly, the Parish Council developed rather an ambitious plan that required extra land, and this could only be acquired by claiming a piece of consecrated land from within the boundary of St. Mary's Church. This matter itself was hugely contentious with public opinion divided, and superstitions abound. However, influential pressure ensured that the acquisition went ahead, and part of the renovated Market Hall was built on deconsecrated land. It is deemed necessary to record with a certain irony that following the completion of the project the town would witness the untimely deaths of three people closely involved with the project – that of the Vicar, the Council Chairman at the time of the decision, and the newly appointed Manager of the Market Hall.

Old Council (For convenience the Cleobury Parish Council elected at the end of the last millenium will be regarded as the Old Council). The supposition of many was that this old Council had a master plan which justified their bold actions and extravagant plans as soon as they took office, but it would emerge there was no master plan, they had simply squandered financial resources, much of it motivated by a desire for popularity. So the old Council soon found themselves in a financial black hole, and they were simply caught red-handed attempting to rob Peter to pay Paul. Yes, it is old fashioned, but a word of advice for anyone making colossal blunders in public life - resign! When they were elected out of office after four years, they left an enormous debt, and a cupboard that was bare.

Bitter reprisals Voted out of office the embittered public figures continued to hide behind a veneer of respectability when they were out and about; but behind closed doors, each month, at every Parish Council meeting they would occupy the public seats with the specific intention of causing as much trouble and disruption as they could by whatever means suited their warped imaginations. It was akin to a 'rent a mob' using foul and derogatory language. Few things are as disgusting as the systemic abuse of power in public office, however, the failure of those in higher Council authority who should have intervened to prevent this nasty course of action, comes close. In the end the sinister aspects of spin doctoring turned Cleobury Parish Council into a political basket case.

John Taylor During the tenure of the 1999-2013 administration, any members of the public who complained or raised concerns about the conduct of that council, were treated with contempt and their concerns were crushed by dissent. It became a nightmarish era with swift and brutal reprisals. This horrid intimidation drove most people into silence; with one notable exception. John Taylor was not deterred one little bit, like a trouper he gallantly stood his ground, he did not succumb to the pressures and hostility; instead remained a valiant and determined critic of this Council, and was a prolific writer to the Shropshire Star.

'Socially inadequate' One vociferous member of that old council was a journalist who was particularly embittered, and became John Taylor's most offensive and vitriolic critic. In March 2004 he wrote to John Taylor and accused him of being 'socially inadequate', 'of having a tenuous hold on reality; of producing slanderous nonsense, and of taking on the role of futile stirring'. But in fact the stalwart actions of John Taylor should be applauded, for his determined efforts had a profound impact. John Taylor was still not deterred by this bully, instead his persistence took him to the head of Legal Services for Shropshire Council, Richard Thomas, a meeting that triggered the appointment of top Birmingham accountancy firm UHY Hacker Young to closely examine the accounts and financial transactions of the troubled council through an Audit. Just the result the electorate wanted, well done John Taylor!

This one is for you, John Taylor: Proverbs 28 v 6 'Better is a poor man who walks in his integrity than a man who is rich and perverse in his ways'.

What drives people to inflict such bare-faced intimidation and unpleasantness? One theory is the classic macho enthusiasm, characteristic of thugs, to revel in power, and to a twisted mind it becomes exciting to be a bully, especially when they escalate their intimidation with the intention of harshly inspiring real fear in the hearts of their critics. Of course their message of intimidation must be spread to provide sufficient political leverage. The values of that group of public figures fuelled only hostility and bred contempt, the concept of supporting cohesion and harmony was completely alien to them.

Poison pen letters The editor of the towns local publication was amongst the embittered group who went to extreme lengths, they even embarked on a campaign of sending poison pen letters and putting up posters etched with skull and cross-bones that circulated within the community, this was a further means of crushing dissent and people became really frightened, an indication of just how bad the political warfare in Cleobury Mortimer had become. It did the town little good that these nasty people were so uncontrolled and ill-mannered, it gave the impression that at least one part of Cleobury Mortimer could not behave itself properly.

Fighting spirit from Jack Castle Jack was a local resident living in Childe Road, a fine upstanding gentleman, typical of those making valiant efforts to confront this political disorder. In a letter published in the Shropshire Star Jan. 2005 Jack wrote 'It is so sad that four Councillors in Cleobury Mortimer decided to resign from the Parish Council. Well, no, it's not sad really – it is totally pathetic. What excuse can they offer to the people who voted them into office? And do they not have the moral courage to see the job through? It is claimed they were clapped by their supporters when they stood down from office; to my mind they should have been booed out of the building. They did not like being a minority on the Council. Well tough, that is what democracy is all about'.

Remembering respected local leaders Many of us can still remember the natural leaders in the communities within this area, in Kinlet there was Michael Dugdale, in Bayton there was Andrew Marsden-Smedley, in Neen Savage there was Eric Ratcliffe, in Cleobury Mortimer there was Tom Pain; with the only natural leader still surviving is George Poyner in Hopton Wafers. Now well turned ninety Mr. Poyner was awarded the MBE for his services to community; both he and his wife Elsie set a superb example of commitment and life-long dedication to community life, and have always been held in high esteem. With these people mentioned it was their natural skills and attributes that enabled them to command the respect of others and to become leaders, and it is essential to mention that they considered their roll to be a social responsibility, with none of them using public office for their own advantage.

An empty pool of leadership contenders Curiously the generation following these natural leaders did not seem to provide us with the same calibre of leadership, and there are various reasons for this, mainly because local politics with diminished responsibility no longer has quite the same appeal, and besides people now prefer to devote their time to a wider range of interests. This creates a problem where communities can no longer rely on the presence of others with standing, and professional leadership skills, like that offered by people who are Head-teachers, Doctors and Policemen who in a different era resided and became well known within the communities they served. The emergence of a void in local leadership created opportunities for those less suited for public office, which has resulted in the situation that blights some local communities now.

SIX

Winston Churchill once said -
'We sleep at night because the police
are there to protect us from harm'.

Around 2002 the Christmas light saga popped up Christmas is a crucial trading time in every town, and Cleobury Mortimer is no exception. The towns around us like Tenbury Wells, Bridgnorth, Bewdley, and Ludlow always have a splendid array of pretty lights, but Cleobury always has the dreariest of Christmas lights, and Christmas 2014 was no exception! These dreary lights do not reflect well on our town, and indicates that this is a town that does not always take pride in itself, a town that is not cohesive, a town that is apathetic, a town that is prepared to accept second-best. This is despite considerable funding; but money is not well spent, and there is a lack the expertise and motivation to ensure that Christmas lights have a greater impact.

The finest example around of Christmas lights must be in Bromyard, where the lights are regarded as amongst the most significant in the country for a town of its size. Indeed, Bromyard lights have their own web-site, and after 30 years' experience that town is able to demonstrate what can be achieved when a strong community spirit is cultivated. Volunteers spend weeks creating the dramatic lighting features and erecting the complex cable structures, which each year culminates into a special switch on day with the streets packed with joyous crowds, marveling at the lights and the superb window displays in all the shops. It is examples like this that frustrate, and emphasis that Cleobury Mortimer, blighted by the conflict caused by so many egotists is rendered incapable of rising to any special occasion.

Trouble looming Cleobury's Christmas street lights were being kept in a store shed at Mumfords, and in the autumn of 2001 along came a jobbing gardener with his clipboard and declared that on behalf of the Chamber of Trade he was changing the plan for lights that year, there were to be no lights at all on the south side of the street, only the north side, and the lack of proper answers to this daft decision only increased confusion. At Mumfords we saw red – and the Cleobury 'Christmas light saga' was triggered. We at Mumfords insisted the lights would remain under lock and key unless they were erected on our side the street as well; letters threatening legal action poured through our letter box. But at Mumfords we remained resolute and advised the Chamber of Trade that the lights remained locked up, with the key kept securely tucked into an ample cleavage. This had the Chamber of Trade men jumping up and down in rage, but it was inconceivable to even consider relenting to the unreasonable demands of a jobbing gardener, a journalist and a trolley collector. Their silly threats and bullying ensured they were treated with the contempt they deserved.

The need to ban nasty-natured people By now the culture of 'nasty-natured' people was beginning to emerge, and those with these particular characteristics were easy to identify. So, as we at Mumfords value our customer base, we had no intention of tolerating them in our shop, it would be inconceivable to do so. So for those involved in provoking trouble or aggravation in any way, within the community, then that was that. The first to be booted out was the jobbing gardener together with his clip-board, the next was to be a rather pompous book-trader. This particular incident happened at a time that followed severe weather that brought down power-lines, so with no electricity in the town our shop was busy providing emergency provisions, when the bespectacled gentleman eased his way up the queue towards the counter; just as instruction were given to staff that the chap holding the old paraffin can was not to be served. 'You, can't do that, you can't refuse to serve me!' he chirped; 'But we have just done so, now kindly do not cross our threshold again', was the response he received, and we have never relented. This trading establishment has continued to exclude those who have been troublesome in one way or another. The firm stance adopted by Mumfords followed sound advice provided by Mr. Marsden-Smedley from Bayton; an exceptionally fine gentlemen; who once said that he found from his experience that: 'If you are ever crossed by anyone, you never give them a second chance'. Advice that has always been heeded.

No political interests At Mumfords we had no interest in politics, always assuming that those elected to represent us in Governance be it locally or national do so with the best of intentions and always with the utmost integrity; so in recent years it was completely unexpected that Mumfords should at times find itself embroiled in political controversy; controversy that has had a deep social and economic impact on our community, and this is how it happened:- The firm stance adopted by Mumfords over the Christmas lights saga came to the attention of two elderly local respected gentlemen, who, during the summer of 2003 asked if it were possible that we could take an interest and observe the proceedings at Cleobury Parish Council meetings. The suggestion was declined citing our lack of political interest; however, with a hint of desperation the gentlemen persisted, and it was agreed to attend just the one meeting.

Stunned disbelief However, it took just that one Council meeting to leave us speechless with shock as we listened in stunned disbelief to the harsh and vindictive exchanges that emerged from a chaotic situation. There are no words strong enough to express what went on that night. This was an insight into a very murky world, where we watched as people we thought we knew well, and had respected, were now behaving like vicious thugs behind the closed doors of the those meetings. These people were supposed pillars of our community, portraying a dark and sinister side to their characters, they had been members and supporters of the Old Council who were trying to intimidate and harass the New Council to trigger resignations and thus a new election.

Turbulence on many fronts Whilst some could consider this fracas of political feuding to be entertaining, and particularly to outsiders who were only observing, then maybe it was, but the serious consequences of this civil warfare were deeply worrying. All one could do during this mad, mad time was to withstand and observe. With deep concern for the people who were the victims in this melee, the natural response was to wade in, to the delight of some and the fury of others; so attendance at most council meetings for the next decade became the norm, just quietly sat observing proceedings from the public seats, and taking note. The old Council remained an embittered rump who wanted to settle old scores, and save their own skins and to do it whatever the cost.

Decade of deceit had begun Despite the horror of the vicious squabbling the newly appointed Chairman Don Griffiths was powerless to respond, he was a good man, but his efforts were curtailed by the presence of the local journalist' who miss-used his influence to ensure that all local papers like the Bridgnorth Journal and Shropshire Star were fuelled with false reports. The hostility intensified, and the pressure directed against the new Council continued to be extreme. The irony of this is that we were already familiar with many of the teachers from The Lacon Childe School, we had even been involved with catering for their social functions in their own homes, some of them we had even considered as friends, yet here they were behaving like nasty-natured feral bullies, we became ashamed of our association with this calibre of folk.

So where did the problems begin? The Market Hall restoration was an ambitious project undertaken by the Old Council of 1999, it entailed the expenditure of over £400,000 on a property with an ultimate value of about £350,000. It would emerge much later that the Council members in office lacked strong enough business credentials and financial restraint to manage a project of this magnitude. It was like watching a catastrophe unfold that was going to end up with a huge negative impact. Establish the availability of any grant-funding and people can become incentivised to arrange their affairs around claiming it, thus developing the tendency to spend more than they would normally. And so it was, despite the grant funding the Market hall project was soon deeply in debt; however, instead of being accountable and honest, the Council resorted to a cover-up and deception policy.

Their priority in office had been to court popularity, rather than focus on financial acumen. This was also reflected in the way that tenancy agreements had been drawn-up; as tenants had been found to occupy the newly-restored building, but the rents agreed did not cover the day-to day running costs. The situation became an embarrassment as a pigs-ear was made of just about everything, it would have been honorable and appropriate for the imposition of the old fashioned virtue, mass resignation.

Decided by the ballot box The election in 2003 brought necessary change, with most of the old Council failing to get re-elected and this enabled a shift in majority that left the old Council in a minority and out of control. They were reeling and responded so viciously that many of the problems facing the town today are a legacy of that bitterness, because the ballot box also determined a necessary change in the county council. Ironically, many of us were at the Metropole Hotel, Llandrindod Wells, following the funeral of Rev. Robert Horsfield on May 2nd 2003 when news was received that confirmed the county election results, quivers of shock went round the room that afternoon.

Thank you, Don Cleobury Mortimer owes Don Griffiths an enormous debt of gratitude, he was urged to intervene in our local politics and when he did the aggressors were eventually defeated. Thankfully, that election result brought change to the Parish Council, and Don Griffiths from Castle Toot was elected as new Chairman. Arriving like a knight in shining armour Don set about the difficult and complex task of righting many of the wrongs of the previous four years. An entrepreneur and businessman, his natural skills and talents, coupled with his strength of character and charisma made him the most successful and effective chairman Cleobury Mortimer has had in decades. Don used his natural leadership skills to the greatest effect, his contribution was as significant to our town, and as comparable to that of Winston Churchill when the country needed him most. Don's sharp mind and intellect sent the vermin scurrying back to their holes, his valiant and stalwart efforts were effective in 'turning around the tanker' that was the huge financial black-hole inherited from the 1999 council. Not one to mince words he brought forth some rather salty language, this town had to stand aside for a man who knew where he was going.

The legacy of Don's Chairmanship is that he brought strength of character and an authoritative approach and coupled these with old fashioned values to deal with an extraordinary situation. The success of his tenure soon restored Council meetings to the dignified occasions they should be, and helped to restore the integrity of Cleobury Parish Council. This period of calm would last just a few years, because lurking in the shadows was more big trouble.

Stranglehold During his tenure the Council Chairman Don Griffiths, was blighted by the antics of rogue journalism, which was by now securing a stranglehold of this town; through the towns administration, its trading community, and through publications owned and monitored by the council. However, during the Cleobury Mortimer civil war that followed the election of 2003 the publication and its editor were found by the Parish council to be peddling propaganda by submitting false information to the electorate and to other local newspapers.

Mumfords offer a helping hand At the time the use of Mumfords shop windows was the only means for the Council Chairman to relay serious parish matters to the electorate and the public in general. Some considered the use of window posters to be melodramatic, and maybe it was, but sometimes melodrama is what it takes. The first window poster appeared in September 2003 and was picked up the Bridgnoth Journal – who reported that Council squabbling had triggered the need to produce the message 'Is the public aware of the attempt to destabilise the new Parish Council'. The only people offended by the notices were those involved in causing the trouble in the first place, the public welcomed the notices, and expressed gratitude for bringing matters to their attention.

An appropriate intervention Early in 2004 Shropshire Council solicitor Veronica Calderbank kindly agreed to come to address the Cleobury Council, the objective of her visit was to try to improve relations, to encourage Councillors to adhere to the code of conduct to be more respectful towards each other, and to encourage a change in attitude, and the need to cultivate mutual understanding, and a spirit of compromise instead of hostility. Despite her best efforts, the message from Ms. Calderbank fell on deaf ears 'There is no one as deaf as he who does not want to hear'. Ironically Ms. Calderbank later became town clerk in Ludlow, where she herself became subjected to unpleasantness so extreme that she left the position. What makes people in public life become so unpleasant?

Thank you Major Coles The political warfare in Cleobury Mortimer became well known, it was making the town a laughing-stock when in Jan 2005 Ludlow Civic leader Major Adrian Coles suggested that with public figures in Cleobury Mortimer at loggerheads, he would attempt to mediate, and offered to broker a peace deal between the feuding factions. He stressed the need to end the bickering and to restore the towns damaged reputation, but nothing seemed to come of his offer.

Oh dear! Oh dear! One notice in our shop window which stated that the Bridgnorth Journal was being supplied with false journalistic reports, came to the attention of the police, and involved a rogue police officer and then a Ludlow Inspector whose response established that they were both open to corruption. It is likely that a Ludlow Police Inspector was acting under pressure, but the question remains, where was the pressure from. The pressure to act in this way must have been intense and it was suggested that it was most very likely the Freemasons who were pulling rank! It is claimed that a Freemason is committed not to testify truthfully when another Mason is in trouble so it is fair to say we could be forgiven for struggling to believe a word that any Freemason had to say.

Maybe the Ludlow Police Inspector was pressurised by the Tory controlled County Council, either way he lied, produced a false report, then he lied again in a cover-up. There was a time when such a thing would be inconceivable, but senior police officers betraying their profession has become common-place, and on this occasion there was failure to co-ordinate police contempt and council complacency with responsibility. Maybe it is time to remind West Mercia Police Force that our expectations of those in public office are far higher than the quality of the service that some police officers are inclined to offer.

Police corruption The law breaking the law has very serious and unpleasant consequences, but then the scandals in Cleobury Mortimer say a lot about how the establishment works nowadays. Yes, there was a level of expectation, but the experience was not met.

Quote from Napoleon Bonaparte comes to mind 'Never ascribe to malice that, which is adequately explained by incompetence'. Incompetence is the safest fallback position for the police force, because the alternative, in systemic corruption and abuse of power at the highest level is too awful to contemplate.

Police Commissioner We have met the newly appointed West Midlands Police Commissioner Bill Longmore several times, he first introduced himself by saying refreshingly that 'He was an old-fashioned policeman with old-fashioned values'. There has never been a greater need to return to those old fashioned values to restore public confidence. We admire the way that he is trying to make a difference, his pragmatic approach is most welcome.

Winston Churchill once said: 'We sleep at night because the police are there to protect us from harm'. That is unless you live in rural South Shropshire where you may not necessarily be quite so fortunate to encounter a gallant policeman when you needed one.

Our police expectation The public expects the police to act with honesty and integrity, at all times. It is simply wrong for those in authority to misuse their powers in a politically calculated way, particularly on threadbare grounds. In the interests of fairness and transparency police intimidation must be challenged. We are disturbed by the prospect of shadowy figures, bent cops, and the growing stench of police corruption. Corrupt officers obstruct the quest for justice, so they must be rooted out. No police force in the world is immune from criticism if it is acting in a politically biased and partisan fashion which is both contrived and malicious. A Home Office report on historic police scandals compiled to restore public trust found 2000 corrupt officers suspected of tipping off criminals, stealing, fabricating evidence, hiding evidence, intimidating witness's and using power to get money and services. There are horrendous cases like that of Private investigator Daniel Morgan who was murdered with an axe in 1987 allegedly as he tried to blow the whistle on rampant police corruption. Local leaders of the police need to be open and honest with the public, which is something they have sometimes struggled with in this part of South Shropshire. Economic cuts should not deny us the police protection that we are entitled to, it is quite, quite wrong that some forces have given up on every day crimes, and do not bother responding. What about the principles of justice? So, come on West Mercia Police Force, shape-up!

Let us touch on Police expectation Most policemen regard the profession as a vocation, a chance to make a difference in society, or to the quality of people's lives; and so it was refreshing to hear of the comment made by Sir Kenneth Newman in 1985, when as Commissioner of Metropolitan police he stated that it was the duty of a constable when exercising police powers to: **'Be seen and to be seen to be seen; unfettered by obligation, deciding each issue without fear or favor, malice or ill-will'.** These principles are as solid today as they ever were. The need for the police, either as individuals or as a service, to not only do the right thing, but to be seen to do the right thing remains at the heart of police confidence and trust. So why are there so many scandals associated with Police officers? Hillsborough must surely be one of the worst.

The Hillsborough tragedy report This report makes disturbing reading. Hillsborough is rated as the most serious tragedy in UK sporting history. On April 15th 1989 at the Hillsborough Stadium in Sheffield for the FA semi-final between Liverpool and Nottingham Forest, a human crush resulted in the death of 96 supporters with a further 766 being injured. The corrupt actions of the police turned the tragedy into a high profile scandal, with the police distorting the truth, and refusing to concede they may have been at fault. It is testament to the traumatised families and the tenacity of their long campaigns for justice and truth that these revelations have emerged. Evidence was fabricated and misinformation spread to avoid blame. Questions are now being asked about the thoroughness of the investigation, and the conclusions that were reached. For his part the conduct of Chief Constable **Sir Norman Bettison** beggared belief. The disaster was tragic enough, but the IPCC - Independent Police Complaints Commission made the comment 'The Hillsborough disaster and its aftermath have become synonymous in the public consciousness with allegations of police attempts to cover-up the truth, and to manipulate and deflect blame'. Bettison faced investigation relating to allegations he played a key part in this; in addition claims also emerged that he had similar involvement in misconduct by obstructing justice in the Stephen Lawrence case. Relatives of Hillsborough victims endured intimidation by police officers.

Hillsborough justice for victims Chief campaigner - Ann Williams. The travesty of injustice, coupled with lies and indifference, prompted Ann to establish the campaign 'Hillsborough justice for victims' where she became one of the loudest voices; brave and tenacious, she has been hailed as the ultimate inspiration to womankind, but sadly Ann passed away in April 2013. Her efforts were acknowledged by the BBC at the Sports Personality Awards in 2013.

SEVEN

Winston Churchill - 'Always be guarded against tyranny, whatever shape it may assume'.

Back to local politics The Market Hall restoration saga was swiftly followed by the Market Towns Regeneration Grant saga which entailed the potential of £500k match-funding grant aid for the benefit of the community. This proposal again created controversy within the town. When the community was asked what projects it would like supported, a functioning swimming pool was considered the most favoured option, with either the pool already in the town to be brought back into use; (this was a pool that had been paid for by public subscription), or the provision of a pool in conjunction with the Pioneer Centre, in Neen Savage. It was claimed that a swimming pool would appeal to the wider community, those not suited to the running track or the rugby team. Considering that The Lacon Childe School had been given sports college status, this did not seem an unreasonable request.

An elaborate charade However, what the town's residents said they would prefer, is not what the authorities said they could have; so this was followed by a series of lavish public consultations, which did nothing more than bring to the fore the questionable manner in which statistics are presented. In fact the whole thing was an elaborate charade to cover-up a pre-determined decision. Political apathy is a major problem in this town, and it is indicative of, and reflected by, the manner in which public opinion is always over-ruled by Shropshire Council, and in this case, those who were managing the Market Towns Regeneration scheme; so is it any wonder there is apathy? The public is entitled to think, what is the point, or why bother to take interest? So it was, despite the public preference, the books were cooked and the statistics were manipulated to produce the result that suited the developers and Shropshire Council. Boy, what another scandalous waste of public money!

Not paved with gold The streets of Cleobury Mortimer are not paved with gold, but they are paved with very smart York stone at a cost of over £400k! The finished result was not profound, it was hardly noticed, simply because there was nothing much wrong with the original pavements; even the contractor considered it to be a squandering of public resources, adding that it is the cost of York stone which means it is only usually used in prominent city centres. So the focus of the Regeneration Grant went on smartening up the pavements! It is worth just mentioning, that we are now in 2015 and a shortage of public money means Cleobury Mortimer and this part of South Shropshire has had its public services sliced, does not have a police station or even a police presence!

Ken Reynolds Ken is amongst the kind of people who makes this world a better place for the rest of us. Ken served on the Parish Council, and during the darkest days that Cleobury Mortimer politics has possibly ever encountered, the period in 2004 when the harassment and intimidation became so extreme, Ken Reynolds mentioned that he was going to put his house on the market and move away, he had become worn down by the political war-mongering, and the death threat posters that appeared around the town with his name on them were just too much for him, they were the last straw. But we at Mumfords suggested: 'Don't do that, it would be like giving in to tyranny, and that must never happen. Hold in there Ken and wait and see if the situation can be turned around'.

The situation was turned round and the tyrants were defeated.

Following the election of 2007 Ken Reynolds went on to become Cleobury Parish Council Chairman, but Ken was approaching seventy and said it would be his last term in office. By the time of the next election he would have served forty three years continuously on Cleobury Mortimer Parish Council, eleven years as Chairman and four years as a District Councillor. Ken came from industry having spent many years in the carpet trade, where he also served as a trade union steward. Hence, Ken has never exploited public office, instead he used his position on the Council to enable the working class and those less fortunate to have a voice. It has been observed that Ken Reynolds would have done more to help vulnerable or needy people in this community than any other person; he has done this discreetly, entirely without fuss, and he never ceases to use any opportunity to help others whenever he can.

This true sense of community spirit and generosity was also a characteristic of his late wife Sandra, who likewise gave generously of her time and her efforts to help other people, expecting nothing in return. Sandra spent over twenty years leading the local scout troop. Nowadays, there is little evidence of community spirit in the main street of Cleobury Mortimer, but there was plenty of it tucked away in a cul-de-sac off Furlongs Road. In recognition of the struggles that Ken endured whilst he was a Parish Councillor, the hostility, the intimidation, the ridicule at his lack of articulacy, (Ken is a man who does not do fancy talk, he calls a spade a spade, and tells it how it is); we made Ken a special friend of this retail establishment.

The Under-dog With further irony it had been claimed that Ken Reynolds, the plain speaking socialist ex-trade unionist was the 'bad boy' on the Parish Council. Yet from all the years that we sat in the public seats at Council meetings we are able to confirm that it was Ken, who told the truth whilst serving in public office, and always put the interests of the community first; whilst we observed that it was the egotist and the self-styled pillars of our community and the retired teachers from Lacon Childe school who were corruptible and exceptionally nasty natured. This prompted a decision to consider favouring the under-dog if he ever needed help, as it is most likely that he would be the one deserving support and the one most likely to be truthful.

Living life to the full We recognise Ken's rather unique qualities, there are not many of his advancing years that live such a full, interesting and colourful life. Always prudent, Ken has a knack of securing the best seats in the best enclosures at the best sporting fixtures at the most reasonable cost. Ken is here, there and everywhere following racing and sporting fixtures nationwide, with what must be the most remarkable list of connections. Having such an extensive and intriguing sporting social circle helped Ken to rise above the local political furore that he endured from the riff-raff he encountered at so many contentious local Council meetings.

Leaving a legacy In a typical manner, Ken declared in 2011 that before his political retirement he wanted to do one last thing for the town; that was to use his position as Council Chairman to ensure that Cleobury

Mortimer had the best value from the Muller land deal. But as always the unexpected is lurking around the corner, and in this case, more political corrupt practice was about to peak above the parapet.

What is the motive behind corruption? Is it money, money, money and always money? Sometimes life seems to be a Pandora's box of corruption, that has permeated every facet of society; but all corruption must end now. We need a brave new world where people strengthen their courage to do what is right, and fight corruption within society; we must go on 'corruption watch', and help others to resist the temptation of corrupt practice. We must influence by raising our game; lead by example, set a bench-mark, draw a line in the sand, and show that crossing the line risks going from good to evil.

More trouble looming The first indication of more trouble looming, happened by chance, it was after a civilised meeting of Cleobury Mortimer Parish Council in February 2012, when several of us gathered in the pub for a chat. It was close to midnight, when a bespectacled public figure, often considered a schmoozer of galactic proportion, appeared to be rather inebriated as he suddenly blurted out 'Watch this space, a political coup has been planned, and everything on the Parish Council is going to change direction, Ken is to be booted out of office'. In the mold of a typical egotist, this public figure had never been elected to the Parish Council, instead he was one of those co-opted into a vacant seat; and came with questionable credentials, as did another egotistical political traitor; the other guy propping up the bar that night; had not been elected either, but also had been co-opted some months earlier. These two traitors were aiming to rule the local political roost, by foul means rather than fair!

That was way out of order It ill-fits anyone to impugn the honour of a Councillor who has served the community valiantly for so many years, without expectation of recognition or reward. And so it was, on March 16th 2012 Ken Reynolds was ousted from the Chairmanship by an alliance determined to destabilise the Parish Council through a blood-less coup; an act that was supposedly engineered by a prominent public figure in order to manipulate the sale of the Muller land as part of a dodgy property deal. Ken had to be ousted because he did not have a corrupt trump card up his sleeve; he just had a far better offer on the table from a developer prepared to pay £535,000 for the Muller land; a sum that would have been a huge benefit to Cleobury Parish Council, which had no assets of its own.

End of an era for Ken And so Ken's forty three years public service to Cleobury Mortimer, was ended by a bunch of local conniving political crooks. Ken rose above the furore, he refused to attend another Council meeting, and then at the end of his term he did not stand again for re-election. The political reputation of Cleobury Mortimer Parish Council was tipped over the edge into the moral cess-pit where it remains to this day.

EIGHT

Winston Churchill - 'The further back you look, the further forward you are likely to see'.

More public figures with questionable credentials The approach that the newly installed members had for public life was not so much the need to serve the community, more the lust they had for power and kudos, which came with little semblance of accountability. Having been co-opted to public office their inexperience and unfamiliarity with public life was immediately apparent. A new style of leadership had arrived that did not come with occasional erroneous over-sights, but instead the new approach reflected a deliberate move to ensure transparency and accountability no longer factored. Sat in the public seats at his first meeting were two past Council Chaiirmen who witnessed the new administrative team make comments and approve decisions that were then falsified and recorded inaccurately in the minutes. This had never been known to happen before, a previous Clerk had been Eric Mark, whose conduct over many years had always been exemplary.

Changes were sweeping into the local administration that gave an insight into a very grubby world; for the new team brought with it a culture of sleaze, corruption and cover-up. In fact some of the new public figures claimed to have come from the business world, so this aroused intrigue about what sort of business ethics had they been involved with. Their experience in public life had been limited, so it is quite likely they considered that finding themselves suddenly influential in public life was like taking over a new company, you just go in there and do your own thing, put your own stamp on everything, and wow betide anyone who challenges your actions. Public life is not quite like that, it is a position of responsibility, there is need for accountability and transparency; there is a code of conduct to adhere to, and protocol to follow

Too relaxed an approach It has been mentioned before that local government had a more relaxed approach to instilling the code of conduct which offered carte blanche to those in the mold of modern political figures to be as dodgy as they liked without accountability. Government officials were lacking inquisitiveness about issues raised, procedures should have been tighter than they were, given the seriousness of many of the allegations. The usual practice when any type of malpractice is identified is to nip it in the bud before it takes hold, but local government would not respond appropriately; so it became a downward spiral, with others being coerced into the same dodgy political process. An attempt was made to record meetings but the newly appointed administration would over-react and became extremely agitated whenever they suspected a recording device was in the room.

A staged political conspiracy Cleobury Council meetings began to reflect a classic example of a modern political class demonstrating no discernible character, political talent or integrity, beyond the need to bask in reflected glory or engage in political stunts, there was a distinct absence of any strategic thinking. This new administration talks about the money that has been acquired during their tenure, but not about the huge amounts of it that has been lost. The devious strategy to appoint this new controlling administration mid-term was part of a staged political conspiracy to engineer the transfer of a valuable piece of parish land into the hands of a private development company. Financial articles in The Telegraph and The Times had at the time highlighted that health care was the most lucrative form of investment, so there was much at stake, and it was certainly worth shafting the electorate for. At the time a TUC report had revealed that the income of medical practioners had risen 153% compared with that of a baker at -1%.

How The Muller land deal unfolded Where money is to be made, fraud is never far away. Now, whenever a logical argument is explained, most of us have no difficulty in accepting its merits, however, with the Muller land deal, no logical argument was explained, because there was no logic behind the dodgy proposals. The whole land-deal was rigged from the start, with logical argument being replaced by a farcical series of public meetings which were all based on distributing misleading data and propaganda.

The first public meeting was held in St. Mary's Church, what better way to give credibility to a rigged proposal than use a place of worship! But the mass of people present did not really understood the significance of what was happening at the time, they had no concept that they were being used to justify a political conn job. The format for all the public meetings held, focused on a 'rent a mob' style that provided the cheerleader chorus for the bully-boys whose undue influence was directed at the public with a complete lack of propriety, transparency or realism.

Lynch mob So it soon became established that not all lynch-mobs were propping up tyrannical regimes in third world countries, there was a lynch-mob right here in our town. Its primary function was to stamp out any resistance, and to propagate panic and hysteria through confusion and ignorance; whilst dodgy public figures focused on contradictions, deficiencies, misinformation and illogical conclusions to ensure that nothing else mattered but ratcheting up pressure, whilst playing to the impressionable folk seated in the public gallery.

Bullies in the local health service The manipulation continued beyond the meetings, and was directed against anyone who dared to question the logic of what the local health service was up to. Residents in Cleobury Mortimer became frightened into silence because anyone who dared to question the bizarre 'goings on' would find themselves black listed, unable to get medical appointments, and were even blocked from moving to other surgeries. Any complaints that people made were immediately rebuked. We at Mumfords were not alone in feeling uneasy and very disturbed about what happened in the health service in this town during that very disturbing era; which came at a time when shocking NHS scandals from all over the country were just emerging.

Many dodgy dealings and the questions that need answering The Muller land deal exposed a dodgy political system, influenced by many public figures in particular. It exposed all that is bad about human nature; and it exposed just how naïve and easily misled the electorate can be. One influential public figure involved at that time was a Shropshire Council Cabinet member an absurd title for a local functionary, but it was clear the extra power had gone straight to their head. The private development company involved in the project had a portfolio of £130 million; a value not accumulated without using a certain amount of 'sharp practice', and the exploitation of any opportunity particularly within the public sector.

- The Private Development Company looked at ten prospective sites around Cleobury Mortimer on which to build a new medical centre, all the sites were at market value of around £500k. Was it unsurprising that they preferred the site they could secure for just £104,000?
- Why were details of the offer of £535,000 for the land from Bovis kept from the public?
- The Muller land became the sole property of Cleobury Mortimer Parish Council, so with public money involved, why was a stronger negotiating stance not used?
- Why has it not been entirely clarified why a private development company could be allowed to exploit a situation to such detriment?
- A new medical centre was required to serve the increase in patient numbers from the surrounding ten parishes. Why did those 10 parishes not contribute towards the new medical centre, particularly as Cleobury Mortimer is not an affluent community?
- Why was a public meeting held with residents from the other 10 parishes present, who all voted to influence a decision to be taken by Cleobury Parish Council?
- Why was the comment made as hands were counted: "I don't care if they come from Timbuctoo as long as they all put their hands up"? This is not Democracy, this is political sleaze.
- Why did the Unitary Councillors whip up hysteria and a frenzy at a public meeting by making false public claims?
- The decision did not reflect wise judgment, would any other local land owner be coerced into selling a valuable site under such circumstances?
- The old medical centre was in negative equity, did this reflect poor financial management?
- Was public money used to top-up the shortfall in medical centre pension pots?
- Why did a Unitary Councillor obstruct consideration for the old medical centre to be exchanged in lieu of the parish council's shortfall on the sale of the Muller land?

- What are the terms of any lease on the medical centre, and what happens after 25yrs?
- Why did a Unitary Councillor make the infamous comment 'This town is apathetic, they will accept anything?'
- One Cleobury Parish Councillor was a chef living and working in Ludlow at the time, who just popped back for the crucial vote, is this the manner that serious political decisions should be taken?
- Is it correct that this had been an elaborate charade to disguise a pre-determined decision?

The Pied Pipers Public figures involved projected an image of principled consummate leadership, yet built a case on the blurred lines between fantasy and reality; and of course knowing exactly which strings to pull. The whole saga stank to high heaven as they behaved like Pied Pipers whipping up a frenzy of fear and hysteria through propaganda which aroused the normally apathetic electorate into a state of panic and fear, they responded by following the Pied Pipers, like .... sheep!

Fear-mongering is a trick to cajole people into responding in manner that is not always in their best interests. The electorate did not stop for a moment to consider implications or the magnitude of their actions. It is a sad reflection that any election result can so often be determined by whatever sensational headlines hit the news-stands on the critical Election Day.

Propaganda As we know, propaganda is associated with furnishing incorrect information to influence thinking, and we are usually swamped with it around here. Cleobury Mortimer has always been disadvantaged that its location means it is unable to communicate easily with the local population. The Ludlow and Tenbury Advertisers, The Bridgnoth Journal, The Kidderminster Times and The Shropshire Star all cover our town, leaving no publication to be universally read. By contrast The Hereford Times has a circulation of about 30,000 and is regarded as a reliable newspaper read by most households in that county. It is possible that a local publication could be regarded as the publication most read within the Cleobury hinterland. However, the history of this publication and the questionable credentials of its editor determine that it is a propaganda publication. Propaganda is a hugely successful tool for overall submission to state ideology, strengthening a hold on public influence whilst reasserting authority, with challengers getting no chance of news coverage.

The end of an era. At one time Cleobury Parish Council had its own local publication which it owned and monitored, but during the Cleobury civil war of 2004 this publication and its errant editor were found by the Parish Council to be peddling propaganda by submitting false information to its readership and to other local newspapers. In fact the issue No. 124 of May 2003 was an example of the problem; the front page editorial must have been the most brazen piece of propaganda ever written in Cleobury Mortimer; it was political garbage intended for the forth-coming election. Thus, the editor was eventually relieved of his services as editor of the publication with immediate effect and out of vengeance he established an independent publication, which is distributed locally and has continued to be used for propaganda purpose ever since. This fuelled comment that the sole control of distributing our local news was in the hands of an unsubstantial figure who blew with the wind. Why did no one see it coming, and why was he never stopped? For too long this country has tolerated in its midst people who actively work to destroy community spirit and everything that it stands for.

A propaganda rag The only local publication in circulation in Cleobury and its hinterland today is the one established as a propaganda rag to provide a sunny place for shady people; then it became a means of peddling headline grabbing fiction and easily demonstrable falsehoods. Now it is a source of garbage in and garbage out edited by a manipulative manic chancer, with few enjoying such a sleazy reputation. It is rather striking how this rag has thrived and prospered on nothing but sleaze, and certainly under the style of a red top. But for far too long this rogue publication has enjoyed undue influence over our community, spewing out monstrous pieces of libelous junk, in a desperate attempt to tighten an egotistical stranglehold on this community.

Too often the readers of this publication are victims of fraud, simply by thinking they can trust the articles they read, after all, why wouldn't they? They think they can read through the ideological bias and just get the facts, however, it is important to understand how knowledge about current events is produced before relying on it, as there are fundamental problems that create distortions, falsehood, and justify the narrative of those in power. Firstly there is the negative journalist who aligns his belief and priorities with the state, then centres his perceptions on serving the interests of power and influence, and ensuring his close proximity to it. Secondly there is the façade journalist whose intentions are to confirm of the reader their already held notions and pre-conceptions; this will help to ensure that his hard work on plans for world domination will be well supported by his loyal readers.

NINE

Thank goodness we have lovely views in Neen Savage.

The **political juggernaut of corruption moves into Neen Savage** The ink had not dried on the Muller land deal before public figures rolled their political juggernaut of corruption into the nearby parish of Neen Savage. This Parish was to be their next victim, and almost immediately public figures ensconced themselves at the heart of the community and began engineering conflict and division, and as recent as Nov. 2014 they are still at it, sat in at Council meetings endorsing and inciting a campaign of bad-feeling, harassment and intimidation against the traumatised sitting Council. This is eighteen months after the Council was democratically elected! The public figures woefully misjudged the situation in Neen Savage, where they were not successful in exploiting the electorate, as they had done so effectively in Cleobury Mortimer.

Bulldog spirit In Neen Savage the electorate is not as apathetic as that in Cleobury Mortimer, and they refused to be exploited; and demonstrating that mild-mannered people expressing reasonable concerns in a moderate tone are not to be ignored, COPAG - Cherish our Parish Action Group was formed in 2012. This is a protest group established by a group of Neen Savage residents who were appalled at the political malpractice they observed in the parish and their objective was to protect the views of the electorate.

COPAG Such was the strength of their cause five members of COPAG were encouraged to stand for election and all five successfully became Councillors at the poll in May 2013, taking control of Neen Savage Parish Council, with a COPAG member now serving as Chairman. The COPAG victory was a collective triumph, showing what democracy is all about; though the group was unsuccessful in challenging any aspect of the contentious planning application which was heard in spring 2013.

Thank you, Martin Neen Savage Parish remains profoundly grateful to Martin Windridge from Chilton for his stalwart efforts in establishing COPAG. In turn the COPAG team deserve commendation for their fresh thinking that produced the most significant result in Shropshire at the Parish elections in 2013. It was hugely fortunate that Julian Clelford moved to this Parish with impeccable credentials, and a stoicism and fortitude that has enabled him to rise above the furore he encounters whilst serving as Chairman of the Council.

Our countryside compensates Thank goodness there are lovely views in Neen Savage, it helps to compensate for the aggravation in the local politics. Far too often public figures become skilled and devious operators, and such a knack was used to deliberately engineer conflict between the electorate of this parish, and has continued to fuel it to ensure divisions remained deep. Fundamental to the initial conflict was a planning application submitted to develop an empty farmstead off Baveney Lane, Neen Savage. There was nothing untoward about the application at all, indeed it would have been supported and approved; such an application was inevitable, as the property had limitations leaving development as one of the only options.

However, the issue was clouded by the scale of the development, and its location gave rise to concerns that it was an application that might be better served with tight regulation applied. The controversy was triggered, however, by the manner in which the application was being engineered through the planning system, by publicly elected figures; who had the intention of shafting the Neen Savage electorate in order to support the applicant. Ironically, this particular property had been subject to planning before, in 1982 when two attempts to secure planning approval at this same farmstead were made in order to provide local employment opportunity, but both attempts were scuppered by the very same fascist influence that was engineering the application through in 2013 without regulation. However, Neen Savage is a rural parish that has been blighted by the actions of fascists and feudalists for many generations, now the Parish also faced victimisation by political corruption, but the silent majority must never, ever be disregarded or underestimated by the vocal minority.

Raucous bunch As the new COPAG led Council settled into routine, they were about to discover the dark and sinister side of local politics, as they attempted to conduct the business in hand; at each meeting they were put under the most ferocious pressure when faced with a barrage of antagonism from the raucous bunch sat in the public seats; who were intimidating, bawling and heckling; these people responsible were not local yobs, but egotists who form a tyrannical regime and consider themselves to be the local 'establishment'. This included elected public figures and a group that were encouraged to form naturally as saboteurs; amongst them were prominent members of our Church, with one of the key instigators being a particularly embittered ousted local public figure.

Curiously, whenever there has been political trouble in and around Cleobury Mortimer over the years, this particularly embittered person has usually been in the midst of it, his photograph appeared on-line as he sat in a political rally over the Muller land disposal in Cleobury Mortimer, he is a man, a classic egotist, with too much time on his hands, so he is in his element being at the heart of any trouble. This is a man familiar enough with political protocol to know that it was not appropriate for him be voting to influence Cleobury Parish Council, where he is not on the electoral roll; and that his stance demonstrated a breach of what democracy is all about, with his involvement epitomising his willingness to engage in any sort of political corruption!

Political traitor If we had not been present at both Shropshire Council (South) Planning meetings held at Westgate in Bridgnorth during spring 2013, we would never have believed the sequence of events of that followed. Public figures who had been elected to office to represent the interests of the electorate, turned traitors, and during a theatrical performance, a range of fictitious and false claims were made, whilst playing to the planning applicant sat in the public seats; a performance so over-dramatic it was impossible to take it seriously. This was followed by a range of bizarre statements like 'Misleading and distorted information cascading from COPAG caused distress within the parish', what rubbish, the only distress caused within Neen Savage had been triggered by the public figures themselves. There was tension in the room that afternoon, and the atmosphere could be cut with a knife, the other members of the decision making Committee began to look awkward and uncomfortable, it was evident that this was a decision that they were not at ease with. However, on the basis of the performance, the Planning Committee approved the application, despite the objections raised by the Planning Officer and by Highways. There is no limit to the corrupt practice that some determined public figures are capable of.

Neen Savage Clerk's dramatic departure During the summer of 2013 the sitting Clerk at Neen Savage resigned, it was a dramatic gesture, and a confusing sequence of events. But most bizarrely the event was shrouded in mystery and confusion that suggested the peddling of a fabricated version of events was a possible attempt to discredit the COPAG group. There was no prospect that the Clerk could pursue constructive dismissal because there were no grounds, and also, a facility of mediation was offered to enable a return to the position, together with any unreserved apologies if they were considered necessary, but the offer was rejected.

It is quite likely that there may have been cajoling by local fascists to act in this way and that the resignation was contrived to create the impression of crisis. But in fact the resignation had the opposite effect and produced a positive outcome; it enabled the Council to appoint a new temporary Clerk to the position and indeed Mr. Peter Martin has proved an asset, his experience and knowledge, coupled with his strength of character have proved invaluable to the newly appointed COPAG Council. However, some of the recent aggravation at Neen Savage has been triggered by the appointment of this temporary Clerk, with some public figures expressing particular concern, suggesting that they may well be profoundly jealous that the integrity of Peter Martin is far higher than their own.

Sabotage Neen Savage Parish Council made two attempts to appoint its temporary Clerk to a permanent position and both attempts were sabotaged. The third occasion on May 14th 2014 was held was at a closed meeting, where Pioneer Centre staff prevented the saboteurs from entering the building where the meeting was held. Scuppered, the eleven saboteurs then convened to their own meeting, with a publicly elected figure seated centrally within the group. This public figure, seriously breached accepted protocol by then proceeding to give guidance to the saboteurs on the procedure to undermine Neen Savage Parish Council at future meetings.

Neen Savage fascists The saboteurs fall into the category of fascists, battling to exert social, and political control through suppression of dissent on this rural community of around 300. The fascist group has ridiculed, belittled, and undermined the efforts of the democratically elected Council. Fascism is a determination to control the thoughts and actions of members of a community by whatever means, with the use of forcible suppression by exerting strong autocratic control even for peaceful opposition. If the electorate has different views or opinions to the fascists, they are presumed to be wrong, and action is taken to ensure everyone is kept in line, even if it requires intimidation and faked authority. Just who do these fascists think they are?

Neen Savage Parish Council Special commendation to the COPAG controlled Neen Savage Parish Council for their sterling efforts in navigating the Parish out of fascism and into freedom. Their resolve has been combined with determination, active diplomacy, open channels of communication and basic courtesy. A remarkable result achieved despite being subjected to a long campaign of harassment. Well done, Julian.

Well done, girls To Jane Clelford and to Sheryl Spragg, well done, girls. As new Neen Savage Councillors, you have shown enormous courage, strength of character and resilience in the face of extreme adversity. Above all you have shown that good leadership comes from combining the right attitude with common sense. The Parish is proud of you.

Psychological warfare 'Bad attitude' is the contagious problem that has affected Cleobury Mortimer since 1999, and has never been eradicated, and now it is prevalent in Neen Savage. For anyone attending council meetings and sitting in the public seats amongst those affected, it makes your skin crawl, you dread the thought of what you might catch from them. This is psychological warfare and it is hampering everything Neen Savage Parish Council tries to do, but this is not the first time that this Parish has encountered psychological warfare:

Anonymous letters Around the year 1999, Neen Savage experienced another spate of unpleasantness which manifested in malicious anonymous letters being sent randomly to residents within the Parish. In order to establish the likely culprit, many of these letters were taken to a document evidence bureau in Birmingham together with a range of handwriting samples. There, the likely writer of the letters was confirmed with 99% certainty to be a supposedly respected member of our community with connections to the Church and to the Parish Council. The absence of DNA prevented 100% confirmation. This sleazy episode indicates what some rural communities still have to contend with. The incident, offered similarities to the traits of feudalism – in which crude attempts are still made to try to secure a system of hereditary rule over a territory to encompass the social, political, judicial and economic spheres. These people lack natural leadership skills, yet are desperate to instill power and prestige in the community which they define as their entitlement; these snobbish, devious and deceitful folk expect the people to roll over and do as they are told and comply with rigid obligations. Hence even today some communities like Neen Savage are faced with this deep rooted and long standing problem; but we are in the twenty first century and must remember that bullies only respond to strength, so we must all respond accordingly.

Public life bloated by questionable judgment Society is full of people with no scruples who are morally or financially corrupt, and others with no integrity who will never recognise or acknowledge the truth because their own world is based entirely on lies. These people usually form themselves into like-minded groups and close ranks to present an almost impregnable barrier to outsiders. Then we began to direct our observations towards the antics of our local Council and people we elected to serve our interests. Pubic figures are generally central Government puppets whose ultimate ambitions are to transfer their self-serving methodology to high office where they can dip their snouts into the public trough whilst treating with contempt those they claim to represent.

The corruptocracy If good people continue to turn a blind eye to the activities of these parasites, the culprits will continue to prosper. In many cases the law actually protects the culprits, confirming that those who introduce and enforce laws have in their midst some of the most dishonest and corrupt members of society, politicians, ombudsmen and solicitors – known as the corruptocracy. The dishonesty and corruption in politics and society must be brought to account and stopped. Corruption must not be allowed to rule from the top down.

TEN

Aleksandr Solzhenitzn - 'The fine line between good and evil does not run between nations, religions or creeds, but every human heart'.

Social engineering At this point it is appropriate to look at psychology in an attempt to understand what is attributed to the social breakdown in our community. It is claimed that people are easier to manage if they are in conflict amongst themselves, and this probably explains why some local public figures have deliberately stoked conflict within our communities, it has been for their political advantage to have division; in effect they have triggered psychological warfare as a political distraction. What is curious is how people who had always appeared mild mannered and community spirited have had their personalities and characters changed beyond recognition by the tactics used in this game of psychological warfare, turning local politics into a poisonous and dangerous game, with the emergence of a sociopathic culture – the ruthless against the rest of us. Is this sociopathic engineering?

One question that remains puzzling is how much of this action is attributed to the directives and influence from central Government. Shropshire Council has a code of conduct by which each of its public figures is expected to adhere to, which in turn is intended to reassure the electorate that the integrity of public office is always maintained. But why is the code of conduct not strictly adhered to? Why do our public figures regularly and confidently flout the law? Why is local Government so inclined to have a cover-up policy to defend them?

What makes some people in public life become so unpleasant? There is no better way than consider the words of the renowned Russian writer **Aleksandr Solzhenitzn** 1918-2008 "The fine line between good and evil does not run between nations, religions or creeds, but every human heart".

We must surely recognise, not merely the courage and integrity of this man, but also the relevance of his message to our times. He is telling us that if there are evil systems that is because there are evil people, evil intentions and evil states of mind. 'It is to human beings that a call to the better life is addressed, and the best we can achieve through amending the systems of government is to ensure that mistakes can be corrected and evil condemned. But we should not deceive ourselves into believing that the solution to the problem of evil is a political solution, and that it can be arrived at without spiritual discipline and without a change in life. It is only when we recognise the fine line separating good is drawn through the human heart, and that we finally understand the lessons of the twenty-first Century. The conditions are in place for evil to prevail since there is nothing to prevent it, and even in totalitarianism, evil belongs to human beings and not to the system'. Solzhenitsyn is clear that the line shifts inside us as it oscillates with the years, and even with hearts overwhelmed with evil, one small bridgehead of good is retained; likewise in the best of hearts there remains an uprooted small corner of evil. 'It is impossible to expel evil from the world in its entirety but it is possible to constrict it within each person'.

To what extent is this attributed to psychopathy? America appears to lead the research and the debate into psychopathy so it is not surprising that two award-winning books were published by American authors, in 2005 Dr Martha Stoute wrote 'The Sociopath next door', and in 2007 Dr Robert Hare produced 'Snakes in suits- when the psychopath goes to work', both books have helped give the subject more prominence which in turn has enabled psychopathy to generate greater public interest of late.

What is a psychopath and what is a sociopath? Mention the word psychopath and immediately our minds conjure up images of the Yorkshire Ripper and mass murders, but this is a misconception. The term psychopath was first applied to people showing signs of moral depravity in 1900, the term included sociopath in 1930 to emphasise the damage that psychopaths do to society. Considered to be a type of social autism, psychopathy is used to define those who are linked to genetic traits, whilst sociopath is used mostly to refer to people affected through influence and environment.

There are a few things we take for granted in social interaction with people; we presume that we all see the world in roughly the same way, that we all know certain basic facts, that words mean the same thing to you as they do to me; and we assume we have a pretty similar idea of right or wrong. But only now are people beginning to take notice of psychopathy, which is a personality disorder characterised by superficial charm, pathological lying and diminished capacity for remorse, shown through a natural ability to switch empathy on and off. All psychopaths make maximum use of their attributes to deceive and manipulate, and there is no evidence that suggests psychopathy can result solely from social or environmental influences.

Can this type of hypothetic person be identified? He is a text book psychopath, defined by his smile and his relaxed manner, but he is dishonest, devious and manipulative. He pretends to be an empathic listener, but most of the time there is only one person on his mind. He soon ingratiates himself with anyone influential who could benefit him, and invests energy in creating and maintaining a façade that facilitates his career. Then he becomes destructive and dangerous. The public and the law courts have difficulty in appreciating the enormity of the damage caused by social predators like this.

Bad news Psychopaths are very bad news, they are good at hiding their disorder beneath a veneer of normality, they are well spoken, charismatic, manipulative, and use subterfuge, cunning and guile to exert and maintain control, power and a feeling of supremacy over any person or any situation. A psychopath has an allegiance only to himself, if need be he will become a menace and a predator who can suck the life and soul from any person or any community. Psychopaths have the ability to use subterfuge to groom an exploitive group around them in order to create a subculture to help him achieve primary goals. An evil predator, he is faultless and flawless in his ability to turn any situation to his advantage.

When evil walks in our midst it makes all right-minded people recoil in horror Psychopaths do not act in a criminal way, yet they can be as manipulative as a serial killer, and callous with the darkest of intentions. They can engineer destructive behavior, and focus on their goals with a determination to win at all cost, spinning a web of lies and creating complex artificial reality without the remotest sign of guilt; naturally they have no problem with lying under oath. Total control is achieved by creating fear without violence. Psychopaths hang onto their masks with such conviction because they are predators, and besides, they hide behind a façade. They are people so emotionally disconnected that they can function as if other people are objects to be manipulated and destroyed without any concern.

In the work place The neck-tie psychopath wreaks havoc in the office, ruthlessly manipulating and charming their way to the top, calm and fearlessly leading a double-life, with friends and family seeing one person, and other people seeing another side – immoral, perverse, someone who gets a thrill out of defying the law and moral codes. They are cool, self-controlled, and show no remorse for anything they have done, and do not care about anyone they may have hurt, as they care only about themselves. They are bullies, self-absorbed individuals with no conscience, for whom social rules have no meaning, as they are motivated by control and dominance, operating with a grandiose demeanour and an attitude of entitlement. It is hardly surprising that banking is the career that attracts the highest number of psychopaths, and symptoms are most evident in the bankers that are 'high flying'.

There is even a bible reference It is with some irony that the bible makes reference to psychopaths in Proverbs 6:12-19. Things that are detestable to the Lord - a scoundrel and villain who goes about with corrupt mouth, who plots evil with deceit in his heart, he hath haughty eyes, lying tongues, hands that shed innocent blood, a heart that devises wicked schemes, feet that are quick to rush to evil, a false witness who pours out lies, and a person who stirs up conflict within community.

The denial of ultimate malice is our societies greatest weakness Psychopaths consider themselves superior to the rest of us because they do not carry the vulnerability that typically accompanies feelings and conscience, and it is this pathological sense of superiority, a truly malignant narcissism that gives rise to their sense of entitlement to prey on, or mislead others. A psychopath is a very different and dangerous person, which is why it is important to trust your gut feeling when you are in the presence of such predators and to create the necessary defences. Such is the potential impact of psychopathy that it should come with a Government risk warning, to raise awareness, and to enable appropriate response when such people are encountered in societies, or even within families. The existence of evil manifests in destructive and horrific abuse.

Golly gosh - 4% It is claimed that up to 4% of the population could be psychopathic, that is a staggering one in twenty-five people, thus deducing that with the population of Cleobury Mortimer being around 3000 then potentially there could be 120 psychopaths within our community, couple this prospect with the fact that like-minds congregate, and characteristically psychopaths crave power and influence, the leading question emerges 'Just how many psychopaths may be monopolising public life in our town?' The prospect of this became so frightening that there was no way that we at Mumfords would permit psychopathic control of our town without a jolly good fight.

Psychopathic screening Corruption and major problems throughout Government, society and even the world can be traced back to psychopathic individuals. Introducing reform that targets psychopaths will be the only way to get to the heart of the matter, and screening would be of enormous benefit, simply by reducing liability, and ensuring suitability for any responsible position. There has never been greater need for cognitive behavior therapy for those who are naturally manipulative and particularly those who find themselves involved even in local politics. Some aspects of industry are already using a means of psychopathic screening now that advancement in science has provided the facility. Screening would help exclude psychopaths from Government and from all positions of significant power particularly when it is claimed that psychopaths were responsible for the Wall Street financial crash, and also the dramatic UK banking crisis that required a Government bail-out of £900 billion.

Psychopaths and evil influencing society? In any civilised community it is shocking to encounter people so lacking in empathy and so emotionally disconnected that they can function as if other people are objects to be manipulated and destroyed. Advancement in technology has made the world seem a much smaller place, news reports from every corner of the globe can be beamed into our homes in an instant, making us all so much better informed. During 2014, we observed the atrocities in the Middle East, and it prompted our Government ministers, including Prime

Minister and Home Secretary Theresa May to condemn the barbarism and brand the perpetrators psychopaths.

Tyranny and over-coming tyrants A tyrant is always a psychopath, he is a dominant person or ruler unrestrained by law or constitution, he looks to his own advantage rather than that of his subjects and uses extreme and cruel tactics against his own people. With so much aggression within society let's take a look at tyranny; tyranny is nothing but an opportunity for the best in all of us to rise, it is not enough to oppose tyranny, it must be defeated, and when faced with a tyrant be bold or you may as well go home.

Be courageous To secure our free country and our free community, we must struggle through social, economic and physical carnage in a way you never thought possible before. Fear should play no part in our lives, ever, it is far more important to understand the necessity of risk in the pursuit of what is right. Try and understand the nature of a tyrant – consider the prospect that a tyrant you may face is capable of absolutely any depravity in their lust for total control. Be stubborn in your principles and your resolve, but not in your strategies. Stop waiting for others to fight the battle for you, instead blaze trails the tyrants do not expect. Victory over tyranny requires the unwavering will of honourable men; with the defeat of tyranny beginning and ending in the mind. Sometimes these tasks are so epic in their scale one wonders if anyone will step up to weather the storm, but we must strive to open the door to a better society or our community risks cutting its own throat.

ELEVEN

'All that is needed for the triumph of evil is for good men to do nothing' – Edmund Burke

The blight of social media Social media has the country drowning in a sea of vanity, most modern day people have no interest whatsoever in world politics, the potential for harm, or the knock on effect for this country; yet there has never been a greater need to be mindful of global events and their possible ramifications. The rise in Jihadists began ten years ago when Labour allowed them in this country, and so enabling our own communities to be infiltrated by extremism; they are dependent on social media to promote their destructive cause.

Islamic State This is a vicious jihadist movement controlled by tyrants who wish to create a medieval caliphate in modern Iraq, and have unleashed a shocking wave of violence upon ancient civilisations. It has committed the most appalling atrocities – watching is not enough when there is persecution like this, there is a moral and legal obligation to intervene. There are no diplomatic levers to pull or economic sanctions to impose, sadly only the use of force. The questionable judgment of western leaders to support the Arab Spring and so help plunge Libya and Syria into a sea of blood has enabled the launch of Islamic state: an action that suggests the start of the biggest European war since 1945. Now leaders are busy blaming Russia for having the effrontery to defend itself against this new blatant aggression.

Many mornings we wake to shocking headlines During 2014, news headlines suggest that our world is becoming more dangerous and more unstable than we have ever known before, it is crucial to understand that issues that have created the troubling times we read about elsewhere, similarly, can have an indirect impact within our own community. We perceive the Middle East as being a long way from here; but the increasing instability of that region must be looked at in a different perspective now that British born extremist fighters are able to slaughter fellow Brits in the name of Islam. They are amongst the most vicious and callous killers in the region, having become brazen and arrogant; worryingly, their blood-thirstiness means they potentially pose a very real threat in the UK if they return here battle hardened from waging war. A battalion has been created in Britain with the slogan 'It won't be easy, but it will be worth it', against a poster of destruction. An active Jihad terror cell is run from a council flat in Sparkbrook, which is less than thirty miles from here; it should be borne in mind that people from the Sparkbrook area come to our community to work every day.

The Middle East The warning is stark, a battle battleground for a poisonous ideology has formed on the shores of the Mediteranean, turning much of the Middle East into a terrorist state, with ISIS entrenched in a large area. Behind this recent revolution is a toxic combination of surging population, a stagnant economy, authoritarian political culture, deep sectarian tensions, and a festering sense of ant-western resentment.

The warning signs were there Politicians should have known this was coming. In 1994 a controversial article by a US policy thinker argued that far from ushering a liberal utopia, the end of the cold war would be seen as the beginning of something much more dangerous. He added that in the long term crime, over-population, tribalism and disease would make the world a deadlier place, and even then Syria, Egypt and Iraq were specifically mentioned.

An important point is the battle of ideology, with the West having developed democratic freedom, and the Middle East opposing such freedoms and wanting to impose totalitarian rule. Radical extremists want to dominate the entire world; but our own country cannot control its laws and traditions; and so there has emerged rot within and chaos without.

Warmongering can come naturally Our nation needs to set a clear agenda about how we live, and what is expected, no matter what the race, creed or class. Blithe politicians forget that gods of war have been playing their war games for thousands of years, the chaos in the world is not just education and economics related, after all why are violent computer games so popular? Why do the supporters of opposing teams need to be separated in the west's sports stadiums?

Stronger guidelines needed Successful western leaders like Churchill, Thatcher and Franklin Roosevelt spelled out their priorities with absolute moral clarity – a choice between good and evil. History suggests that true statesmanship lies precisely in setting out a moral stance and lifting the fog of ambiguity. There has never been need for leaders of the same calibre – with a clear sense of moral conviction, but also a keen awareness of the balance between caution and inaction; idealism and realism; decisiveness and recklessness.

The wrong impression? Unfortunately our country has somehow landed itself with a generation of political leaders more interested in enjoying their holidays than securing the future of the west; such that one day some future historian may write that even as thousands were massacred in Syria and Iraq, even as rockets rained down on Gaza and Ukraine, even as the world staggered towards anarchy, the most powerful man on the planet was working on his golf swing. Though, maybe Obama and Cameron have seen the bigger picture and consider that they have a better chance of getting a hole in one than leading us all out of the mess we are in.

The Pope speaks out Even Pope Francis has spoken of his concerns, for what seemed like an attempt to use Ukraine to trigger a Third World War. The Pope has condemned the plotters, adding that humanity needs to weep and that war is irrational as it seeks to grow, particularly as its only plan is to bring destruction.

Atrocities in Paris New Year 2015 The start of this year saw atrocities in Paris where radical extremists killed seventeen people whilst claiming an allegiance to Islamic State. The World came out united in outrage, widely displaying the 'Je suis Charlie' slogan in collective condemnation of the death of cartoonists from the targeted satirical publication Charlie Hebdoe. Whilst the claim is that this is more terror from the ruthless Jihadist movement, delving closer it seems the killers were in fact from the local French community, who had been drawn into supporting Islamic extremism because they felt disaffected by society. What happened in Paris for three days should scare everyone. This could happen in any neighbourhood, in any country. Even the prospect that this could be another act under the 'false flag' of terrorism is too awful to contemplate. The term 'false flag' came from the days of wooden ships when one ship would hang up the flag of its enemy before attacking another ship, therefore throwing a false lead as to who was responsible. It is scary to look at the state of affairs across the world and see how many plots are afoot to trigger global conflict of apocalyptic proportion.

The strongest voice The French tragedy was marked by thirty World Leaders joining three million people on a march through Paris which had an enormous impact and media coverage. But the same day one of the most significant comments came from the Moroccan-born Muslim Mayor of Rotterdam who told his fellow Muslims in a statement that was straight to the point 'Muslims who do not appreciate the freedom and way of life in Western civilization, pack your bags and get off back. If you cannot find your place here then vanish'. The Mayor who is known for his no-nonsense approach to immigration added 'If you do not want to integrate then just leave'. This is just the kind of voice we need to hear from all Western leaders, instead of the usual moral cowardice that is often too weak and ineffective.

A wake up call This atrocity in France must serve as a reminder of how fragile everyday life can become. We are reminded that the values that young people learn today do not just shape their future lives, they determine the destiny of our own society. Every community must have a responsibility towards the vulnerable, exploitable and disenfranchised young people in their midst.

Magna Carta –2015 This year will see fanfare and pageantry in recognition of the eighth century celebration of the Magna Carta. The Magna Carta is an iconic document that helped build the foundations of democracy and the rule of law in Britain and abroad. Its greatest legacy is our freedom of speech and our right to question; and to challenge the people and institutions that represent us.

The Charter as it is known, is a document of 3550 words written in Latin. King John was coerced into granting the Charter by his Barons, which forced the King under the laws of the land. Prior to the agreement, which was a peace treaty, the leading Barons had been exasperated at the King's arbitrary rule and high taxes. The Magna Carta outlined basic rights with the principle that no-one was above the law, including the King. The document was lauded for establishing vital principles, and regarded as the foundation document of the unwritten British constitution.

In Chapter 40 the King declared 'To no-one will we sell, to no-one will we delay the right to justice'; the Charter was asserting a fundamental principle – the rule of law; and chartered the right to a fair trial, and limits on taxation without representation. The Charter took root and became a crucial document for England's history. The sealing of the treaty took place at Runnymead, in a meadow on the banks of the Thames between Windsor and Staines on June 15th 1215.

Fundamentally the Magna Carta was associated with the principles of democracy, liberty and human rights; but the Charter also offered a degree of legal protection to Institutions, the Aristocracy and to the Catholic Church, ensuring that any party that stood on a platform that was true to the spirit of Charter could expect be massacred at the polls.

The tragedy of David Kelly The valiant efforts of this courageous man must never be forgotten. He was a humble civil servant who devoted his life to serving his country, he exposed the lies used by the Labour Government to mislead the British public into supporting the Iraq war, thus provoking a disgusting New Labour inspired witch-hunt against him. The Governments cover-up culture will ensure the nature of his tragic death in 2003 will remain shrouded in mystery. Whilst many of us can feel detached from all these issues, as they may not affect us directly, one must never become complacent as the ripple effect will inevitably have an impact on Cleobury Mortimer one way or another; we remain a vulnerable community with no effective police security, and no effective local leadership.

How effective is the Government at protecting the public? Contemplating the influence of psychopathic people within societies worldwide, it is inevitable that the adherence to law and order, coupled with respect for cultures within civilised communities, it is going to need the iron will of strong leadership to implement. The British Government has now called on all local leaders of Muslim communities to use their influence to control radical extremism in an attempt to diffuse the risk posed in the wake of threats made against police officers on duty.

National security The Prime Minister has personal responsibility for our nation's security. History is now reminding us who were the effective leaders in the past. The negative impact that psychopaths have on societies, cultures, economies the world over means that strong and effective leadership is the only means of counteracting any negative or destructive impact. Many situations are not clear cut or easy to define, though news reports determined that Saddam Hussein and Colonel Gaddafi were tyrants, who had to be disposed of, or so we were told. Further analysis is now telling us that as brutal as these leaders were their strong and powerful leadership kept the lid on what would be a far more tyrannical and brutal regime. The complexity of Middle Eastern culture is something that we are only just learning about, but if World War three has started, it will lead future generations to question the calibre of the politicians of today.

'All that is needed for the triumph of evil is for good men to do nothing' – Edmund Burke

Beware of the copy –cat syndrome Days after two decapitations by Jihadists in the Middle East, a lone assassin roamed the residential streets of London looking for a victim before he randomly chose an innocent grandmother and beheaded her. How did we move from a civilised Christian country to the domination of a group so violent and extreme? This situation is vile and terrible, but it must be understood that weakness gives confidence and encouragement to the violent extremists cutting a swathe in our midst. The dangerous situation in the Middle East can only implode on us the need to have strong leadership within our own community, but the outlook for that remains grim.

The Roman Empire – intriguing As society has developed and changed at such a pace one cannot help but wonder what happened at the end of the Roman Empire, and it is intriguing to learn that the Empire fell because it could not defend itself against barbarism. Roman society became apathetic, civic spirit dwindled, and towns began a slow decline, the great boom was over. Attempts to revive the towns was ineffective, the Emperors became dictatorial and ruthless as they aimed to centralize and streamline administration; then attempts to dragoon the people into supporting the defence efforts generated little enthusiasm with society becoming even more apathetic. By 425 AD Britain ceased to be in any sense Roman. The end of empire is always messy, and Roman Britain was no exception. No clear decision to decolonise Britain was made, instead the garrison was run-down over a generation and then the remnant was simply cast adrift to fend for itself, which left the country exposed to barbarism. The years 440 – 500 AD saw civil war and famine in Britain.

TWELVE

Church – so where does the Church stand in our troubled communities?

<u>Does the Church ponder to the needs of those who shout the loudest or flash the biggest amount of cash?</u>

Our culture is forged by Christianity, and we look to the Church for moral authority, but at times the Christian community appears to struggle with example, leadership and direction. We recognise that the body of the Church is the congregation, so a Church can only be as good as the example shown by the congregation, which in turn is guided by the sermons and the influence of the Clerics. Sometimes, situations occur where the tail can be seen to be wagging the dog, it is to be hoped this is not the case in either Cleobury Mortimer or Neen Savage.

During the last decade or so Cleobury Mortimer has had some turbulent political times, but has the Church supported the community enough, or does the Church consider that its function is to support just the Christian community, and to fix the leaking roof?

The Church cannot make the claim that it does not take sides on political issues, when it is the body of the Church that is so often the cause of the conflict in the first place. Church clerics have a responsibility to ensure that errant members of their Church Councils are brought to account when flouting the principles of Christianity within communities. Turning a blind eye is not the approach; come on local Church clerics, learn from the high profile scandals of late that have rocked the Church, resist a cover-up culture and lead by example.

The political conflicts in Cleobury Mortimer and in Neen Savage saw the involvement of people closely connected to the Church, including the

Parochial Church Council and the roll of Church warden, all of whom have been most vociferous with their unjustified attacks on innocent members of the community. Maybe Church members have need at times to look at themselves with a more critical eye. Recent political conflict has done much to establish that better practicing Christians can be found amongst the electorate than those who regularly occupy the Church pews; hypocrisy is the only word that comes to mind.

All Christians are followers of Jesus, and Jesus was not a troublemaker, he always defended good and decent people, and neither was he a bully or an intimidator. The implication is that political corruption is a self-perpetuating monster that consumes anyone who stands in its way; by not blowing the whistle, it is helping to perpetuate a culture that is damaging to everyone.

The Good Old Days – were so much nicer This may be a nostalgic comment, but it is still a very significant one; and certainly applies in this context. Who can forget the delightful Mrs. Ellen Heywood-Waddington, a person who epitomised everything about kindness and warm-heartedness. The Political conflict in our Parishes would never have happened thirty years ago. A time when Rev. Robert Horsfield and Rev. Heywood-Waddington presided over Cleobury and Neen Savage Churches, their leadership ensured the prospect of such conduct was simply inconceivable. In Cleobury Mortimer the question is raised, has the significance of St. Mary's Church been weakened as the use of the Church has changed? People have short or long term memories as required, but why do Christian members of our community appear to be so frightfully good on Sundays, but the rest of the week they are inclined to become a law unto themselves? As we recall what humanity at its worst can do – we are reminded that the holocaust did not just happen, it began with a brick through a window!

Youth project It is necessary to commend St. Mary's Church and its youth project, for the sterling work they do, which has provided immeasurable support and facilities for all young people in the community. Cleobury Mortimer has few opportunities for young people making this youth project a crucial facility. Austerity cuts have affected local transport, resulting in this town having a poor bus service to anywhere, leaving many young people feeling frustrated and trapped.

Rev. Robert Horsfield Many residents will remember the era from 1979 when Rev. Robert Horsfield was Vicar at St Mary's Cleobury Mortimer particularly the time when he was also Rural Dean of the Hereford Diocese, services in Cleobury Church were always memorable and ceremonial, sermons were without exception, thought provoking and stimulating. During each service souls would be replenished by whatever words of wisdom formed Bob's sermon. Bob had leadership quality, he commanded respect, and under his guidance Cleobury Mortimer was a wonderful place. Bob and his wife Freda were hugely respected and much loved within this community, they spent most of their time here living in The Vicarage next door to Mumfords, our hardware shop. Their home was always a hive of activity, a busy place with lots of coming and going; a friendly and caring haven that was very much the heart and the sole of this town.

Choosing a new Vicar When Bob felt that it was time to retire, his loss to our community was huge, and sadly nothing has been the same since. His like has never been replaced. However, in 2001 the process went underway to appoint a new Vicar; the Church community thought the process might be helped by the commitment to prayer; and so it was each Monday at 5pm for weeks before the selection that a group gathered together in St. Mary's Church to pray. Each week every eventuality was covered, praying that the right candidates would apply, that the selectors would make the right decisions, etc. etc. The sessions were both heart-felt and repetitive, no stone was left unturned in the quest to ensure that 'thy will be done'.

When the selection decision was made, the announcement was not met as rapturously as might have been expected; for the appointed new vicar was Curate Andrew Sewell who had served under Rev. Horsfield and was already well known within the community. It was hugely unfortunate, that simultaneous to his appointment Andy should encounter some difficulties in his private life; he was a widowed father of two, with a second wife who had just given birth to their second child, when she was affected by post-natal depression. Coupled with this, Andy was stricken with meningitis and became physically and emotionally drained by his personal life.

It was a daunting prospect to also take on the spiritual responsibility of seven demanding parishes. All Andy needed was compassion and patience;

two commodities that became in short supply within the Cleobury Church community; for it wasn't long before harsh and unfair criticism was directed at Andy and in time he would be effectively hounded out of office.

If we had not witnessed and been part of the prayer campaign we would never have believed the sequence of events that followed; it might have been quite possible that our Lord decided to test our Christian community at St. Mary's by putting amongst them a vulnerable new Vicar, and to observe how they treated and responded to him. The treatment of newly appointed Vicar, Andy Sewell spoke volumes about the sincerity of the faith at St. Mary's Church and the hypocrisy at the heart of it. But the Bishop of Bristol Mike Hill offered a refreshing comment about the Anglican church that has some relevance to the matter, suggesting that Anglicans can have a tendency to be more concerned about the colour of the napkins for dinner, rather than have genuine concern for those with 'complicated lives'.

The Shoe Box scheme The Shoe Box scheme has been hugely successful, and provides much joy for those who deserve it most. However, it bodes a sad reflection that the Church community can have such an obsession with 'filling shoe boxes', when this process can also reveal much about the sincerity of the compassion of some of those involved. This is shown by the way they treat others in their own communities at times; where some 'shoe box fillers' can be observed stirring trouble at Council meetings, often with clicking knitting needles in hand. Political controversy has established that embattled members of the community can at times be in need of protection from some members of the Church, which bodes well for the claim that the Church is accepting of a more desensitive and uncivilised world

Defining Christianity Our culture is forged by Christianity, we look to the Church for moral authority and expect the Church to take a strong line against abuse of other people. The Church is called upon to be a pioneer of a society in which life is lived as God intended, daring to be different and not dancing to the world's tune. There is need to demonstrate courage and to act when faced with dire consequences. It helps to have a clear understanding of what a Christian is. A Christian is a disciple of Christ, one who has been taught to obey Jesus, with The Lord's Prayer and the Ten Commandments instilled at an early age. But faith is formed by a host of influences, with no single set of policies that are universally regarded as Christian because the meaning of Christianity depends on what is considered practical in a given place or time, thus Christians from around the world may disagree on a wide range of issues. For example, the argument should not be about whether or not Jesus rose again, the argument instead should be about how each person lives individually or within a Church community in light of this event.

The Archbishop of Westminster recently suggested that a vibrant Christian community is crucial for acting as a stabilising force, and that Christians bring moderation and a sense of responsibility towards others. A need to protect and promote our communities must be a main objective, and it must not be forgotten that people still look to the Church for moral authority, particularly during uncertain times. So come on Church shape up, and less hiding behind a long list of excuses!

However, Dr Anthony Seldon considers that religions themselves are much to blame for ills in society, having failed effectively to communicate the message of their founders; and for allowing competitiveness, resentment and hatred to fill the hearts and minds of religious professionals far too often.

Sir Anthony Seldon Dr. Anthony Seldon, 13th Master of Wellington College was knighted in 2014 for his services to education and to modern political history. Dr. Seldon frequently writes in the Telegraph about the impact of society on education, and has most recently been involved with establishing 'Action for Happiness', a movement of people committed to building a happier society where the aim is to establish a fundamentally different way of life where people care less about what they can get out of it for themselves and more about the happiness of others, by leading a more virtuous life, with focus on empathy, generosity, resilience and compassion, thus helping to underpin a more meaningful life. The patron of the movement is the Dalai Lama.

We need a more vocal Church We have great need for the Church to be more vocal and to help respond to the pressing issues of the time. Considering that we have had a welfare state in our society for over 60 years why are so many people sick, illiterate, unemployable and aimless? Why with much more affluence are people not happier and more contented?

Why with better education more surveillance, and laws for everything, is crime on the increase and cruelty so prevalent?

Politicians across the spectrum have neglected to stress the importance of the values of people and institutions which binds society together. The obsession with celebrity culture, of money, adulation, fame and exposure should be accompanied by a semblance of responsibility. The spiritual as opposed to the material should be a far more prominent part of the life of each individual; this may well even help the vicious cycle of poor parenting to stop. The values our children learn today don't just shape their future lives, they determine the destiny of our society.

No one put it better than Gandhi:
'Be the change that you want to see in the world'.

Restoring moral fibre During May 2012 a movement was launched in the House of Lords to restore moral fibre; a welcome step as with so many high profile public scandals the fabric of society is likely to be stretched to breaking point if no action is taken. The initiative was launched to restore the place of character in education and in public life. Character used to be ingrained in the British psyche, it was epitomised by the bulldog spirit and saw the country through world wars and national disasters, Churchill must be turning in his grave. Character is what builds good societies; it is taking personal responsibility, showing self-restraint, having grit and resilience, expressing appreciation. Instead, we have a toxic combination of corrosion at the top of society and neglect at the bottom. The political class has been letting us down for years, breaking promises, lying, and consorting with dodgy people.

Where is the example set? Throughout history, man has looked to religious authority for moral leadership during times of crisis but the Church of England is locked in a civil war over abuse; the Catholic Church meanwhile has critically wounded itself by failing to be candid about paedophilia within its ranks. However, Chief Rabbi Jonathan Sachs the most persuasive religious figure in Britain today offers a rare example of moral leadership. It is frightening there are so few people in public life we can admire. Britain has more CCTV camera than any other European country, they deter not only law breaking, but also the heightened risk of being found out. Children used to be taught the difference between good and evil, to do the right thing, because the right things is the good thing to do, but the young are no longer taught about morals and values. Religious education has all but gone from schools, where the core teaching of loving others, telling the truth and doing good in society, came from. Taking this element from schools, and by failing to replace it with strong moral education, you undermine the foundations of good schooling and society. These days' youngsters have a daily diet of dubious celebrities full of excess, violence and infidelity. So there has never been a greater need for character to be placed back at the heart of society.

English culture Britain was renowned for its quintessential English culture, afternoon tea, good manners, dignity, respect and the reluctance to make a fuss. It is not a British quality to complain, anyway in the past there was rarely need to; there was an era when our society was propped up by integrity, honour and soundness. Now the values that epitomised our culture are ridiculed and devalued. All that the country stood for is being eroded away by malpractice. A culture of sleaze has permeated every facet of our society and weak regulation has played a part.

Something is not right We know deep down that there is something not right about our world, in fact, right now it could hardly be worse, but most people spend their time avoiding the position at all cost. The brutal truth that our social, cultural and legal systems are all about making people helpless, then hammering them without mercy; all the time giving the illusion that right prevails. We must all be more assertive to events and issues that impact our lives and communities.

Wise words from Robert F. Kennedy The brother of US President John F. Kennedy was a man of passionate conviction, carrying a message for change for the oppressed; and a message of hope for the forlorn. Here are extracts from two of his speeches which offer a reminder of our responsibilities:

- **Ripple of hope – 1966** 'Few will have greatness to influence history, but each of us can work to change a small portion of events, and in the total of these acts will be written the history of our generation. It is from numerous diverse acts of courage and belief that history is thus shaped. Each time a man stands up for an ideal, or acts to improve the lot of others, or strikes out against injustice, he sends forth a tiny ripple of hope, and these ripples can build a current that can sweep down the mightiest of walls of oppression and resistance'.

- **Quality of life – 1968** 'For too much, and for too long, we have surrendered our excellence and our values for the mere accumulation of material things. Our focus has drifted from the health of our children, the quality of their education or the joy of their play; our focus no longer includes the beauty of poetry, or the strength of our marriages, the intelligence of debate, or the integrity of our officials. It measures neither our wit nor our courage, neither our wisdom nor our learning; neither our compassion not our devotion to family or community. It measures everything in short, except that which makes life worthwhile, and it tells us everything'.

THIRTEEN

No-one put it better than Gandhi - 'The richer
society is, the less community-minded it becomes'.

Health care scandal During 2012 The Telegraph reported that at
Stafford Hospital forty three patients starved and one hundred and twelve
died of thirst while being treated on the ward. This saga exposed the
changed nature of the National Health Service; it became apparent that
not everyone involved in the profession was compassionate and caring. The
scale of excess deaths was horrendous, and not only restricted to Stafford.
The NHS had become such a financial burden that cost cutting had
imposed enormous pressures on staff. We must pay tribute to the sterling
efforts of Julie Bailey for her determined efforts in exposing the scandal
at Stafford, the CBE she was awarded in the 2013 honours list was well
deserved. Stafford Hospital was not alone, similar scandals have appeared
at hospitals and at care-homes nation-wide that revealed that we are no
longer a naturally caring society.

It was no excuse to blame poor facilities, it was hardened attitudes
and the absence of compassion that was the root cause; and of course in
the rarefied world inhabited by the upper echelons of the NHS police and
social serves, no one ever takes the blame and all that matters is that correct
procedures are followed. Though many nursing staff state that they feel
ill-supported by their senior teams. Too many facets of our national life
are getting forever out of control, with a growing under-tone of aggression
making Britain a nastier more disturbing place to live; far from the days
when there was zero tolerance. There is a need to over-turn values that have
failed society; bold and radical changes are needed in these unpredictable
times.

A shift in attitude needed Closer to home, it went unreported,
though it did not go unnoticed that some of the uncaring attitudes and

unprofessional approaches that has infiltrated our health service, had also blighted our own medical service in Cleobury Mortimer. It should never be the case that the best care is reserved for those that make the most noise; but far too often it has been observed that those who suffer most are those who are less inclined to complain or make a fuss. Local health service staff were known to complain that their ability to function efficiently was hampered by the dated and cramped conditions in which they worked; a poor excuse if ever there was one. One only has to look how compassionate medical staff in war zones and third world countries remain committed in the most challenging circumstances.

Public services need fixing The Social Services scandal has unearthed rather a brutal regime where it is claimed that the NHS has a style of management that insists you will do as you are told, you will not make a fuss, you will deliver the targets, or else. It is claimed that if you cross the NHS you are finished; management are career-focused and will happily bury any bad news. One young nurse starting a new job at a small practice was shocked to discover a backlog of hundreds of emails containing details of patient's tests and results that had never even opened, let alone responded to.

Brave response The young nurse turned whistle-blower and complained, she subsequently lost her job; in hindsight she said she did not regret her action, and added 'If you have a moral conscience, you do not have a choice'. In society it is daring to say things that most know are true, but few are brave enough to speak out and say so.

Our chatty customers The nature of our traditional business at Mumfords is that we have some senior aged customers, and chatty conversation will often veer towards health care issues, and during the last decade it was disturbing to hear how many people had serious complaints to recall about the treatment they received from our local health care facility in Cleobury Mortimer; it appeared that if any complaints were made by the patient themselves or by family members, they were dismissed or fobbed off; it also appeared that a group established to represent patients interests has at the times had very selective hearing.

Mrs. Kath Cleaver Whilst the complaints we heard were only 'hearsay', we are in a better position to recall the experience of our Mumfords shop colleague Mrs. Kath Cleaver who will be fondly remembered by many;

a Yorkshire lass, she and her husband were moved to Cleobury Mortimer by her husband's employer; and Mr. Cleaver continued to work at Mawley Hall as a skilled cabinet maker until his seventies. They nurtured simple dreams like many hard-working couples. Mrs. Cleaver was dearly loved and cherished by her colleagues and customers alike at Mumfords, always impeccably dressed and beautifully coiffed, with a cheery disposition, she was a delight to have around. She always had a kind and friendly word for everyone; and a remarkable ability to remember everyone's name, their children's names and their dog's names; a dog-lover, she had a ready supply of dog chews which she freely dispensed.

During thirty-five years living in this town Mrs. Cleaver did not once visit the Doctor, she was not one to make a fuss about anything; however, acute indigestion left her with no choice but to make an appointment, then over many, many months she visited the surgery many, many times. Despite the advice, prescriptions and the treatment dispensed Mrs. Cleaver's health did not improve, it continued to deteriorate. Deeply concerned her family insisted that she seek a second opinion. The second opinion confirmed that Mrs. Cleaver was suffering from advanced stomach cancer, she passed away a short time later; a victim of medical negligence. Mrs. Cleaver, with her hugely generous spirit was badly let-down, and despite the tragedy of her loss, the circumstances have never been acknowledged.

This was not an isolated incident, but all those who suffer have no voice, no-one listens, no one is interested, no-one is concerned. Something as simple as an x-ray can cause enormous concern; following an x-ray it is an anxious time for the patient, but there is even greater concern when there is no follow-up. Too many times the failure to inform the patient of results, can cause huge and unnecessary anxiety. Local Health care can be inconsistent, either very good or potentially neglectful, with patients returning home from major surgery facing a lottery whether they will receive attentive after-care or not.

Why are the elderly treated like Pariahs The elderly have time on their hands, love in their hearts and much wisdom to impart, but the state has made us too selfish to care for our parents. In a broadside that will resonate with so many, it is often asked why todays elderly are treated as pariah's – and one of the paradoxes of modern Britain is that although life expectancy has greatly increased and there are consequently more old people, they are in many ways less respected and valued than they used to be. It can scarcely be disputed that people in their 70/80/90's are increasingly made to feel they are part of a burdensome minority which is more or less surplus to requirement. There is fear that the assisted dying bill will raise the prospect of over-bearing relatives putting pressure on the elderly to do away with themselves for fear of being a burden.

These are examples that illustrate just how much the elderly are increasingly viewed as a soft target for those who believe younger people who have not contributed so much to society should take precedence in so many areas of life. Elderly have more complex needs generally and risk being struck off GP surgery lists, then there has been recommendation that well-off pensioners should have benefits axed to pay for radical reform of Britain's broken care system. Pensioners are asked to agree a 'do-not resuscitate' scheme, what a crass, presumptive and insensitive thing to ask? The NHS has developed a condescending and sometimes callous attitude towards the elderly – after all it was the NHS that operated the now defunct Liverpool Care Pathway without telling the public anything about it.

Muller land deal The health service certainly had no qualms about being ruthless when it chose to exploit the elderly and the vulnerable over the Muller land deal in Cleobury Mortimer. The new Medical Centre is a superb facility, and this part of South Shropshire deserves the best medical facilities that are available. But behind the concept of this project was some very underhand procedures used by a collusion that included the political establishment that ensured that faced with the full force of these heavy-weights, common sense and rationality did not stand a chance.

Distasteful public meetings were called to present a one-sided story, where heckling and exerting undue pressure from a lynch-mob became the order of the day. The now defunct Primary Care Trust which organised health care facilities claimed that big funding was expected to finance a new medical facility, but this did little to explain why they were claiming an unreasonable advantage by demanding to secure the public land so cheaply. Any complaints about this practice were immediately rebuked; wow, and they call this progress!

FOURTEEN

Winston Churchill – 'You have enemies?
Good that means you have stood up for
something, sometime in your life'.

How did we get involved? The question is often asked how we at Mumfords became embroiled in local politics. We ask ourselves the same question every day! But on a more serious note, it would have been impossible for us to observe so much wrong doing in our midst without attempting to make a stance against it. We have observed that possibly one million pounds has been squandered or misused in this community over the last decade, this has occurred through questionable judgment and manipulation of public opinion.

Now, we would not normally be unduly concerned about these sort of matters if it were not able to remember with such clarity the very lean days at the start of the second millennium. This was a time when our Council had no money and even less inclination; Cleobury had become a grubby place as there was no street cleaner; dog-fouling and litter were major problems; flower beds were over-grown and neglected, and the town was generally unkempt. It was a time when there so simply no public money for anything, and besides our town was also in the grip of political civil war.

Disgusting toilets However in 2003, something happened to trigger a reaction from us, and this took the form of a letter that appeared in the Shropshire Star headed 'Beautiful town, but toilet is disgusting'. It was sent by a journalist from Derbyshire would had come to visit this town, and St. Mary's Church in particular to see its twisted Spire. We were embarrassed by the negative newspaper article, so we checked, and discovered the toilets were as bad as claimed. The Council was up to its eyes in debt so there was no prospect of public funding, so Mumfords paid for the public toilets to be cleaned, power-washed and then to be white-washed. 2003 was also the inauguration of our new Vicar, it was a very special event with several Bishops coming to our town. Despite this auspicious occasion Cleobury Mortimer was certainly not looking its best, so Mumfords paid for the flower beds to be tidied up and for flowers to be planted, we wanted the town to be portrayed in a much better light.

The letter sent to the Shropshire Star May 3rd 2003 by Mr. R. Deeley from Derby DE3 said:

Beautiful town but toilet is disgusting

- 'As a visiting tourist to Cleobury Mortimer recently, I must write to express my disgust at the condition of the public toilets in the town centre. On the day I visited I have never felt quite so nauseated, nor witnessed such unhealthy conditions in any town I have visited. I will not offend readers with too graphic a description, but suffice to say that no door was lockable, they were unclean, walls were dirty and displayed graffiti and some toilets were unflushed. Cleobury Mortimer is a beautiful old town and much publicised. I was told that many similar complaints had been made, and the state of affairs had existed for some years.
- How does this affect local trade's people in the town, and what sort of image does this project and particularly to over-seas visitors? How many, I wonder have had a similar experience, and moved on quickly, and did not bother to visit shops or eating places that are both very clean and welcoming. In conclusion I think that this disgusting facility in the sorry state it is in, could have an adverse effect on the otherwise excellent publicity this lovely old town deserves.
- Someone must take responsibility and discharge that situation'.*

Remembering lean times So remembering the impact of those lean times, we at Mumfords recognised that the Muller land deal offered a golden opportunity, with revenue from the sale becoming an asset of the Parish Council, which would help the community when lean times return. Cleobury Mortimer is not an affluent community, the Parish Council does not possess reserves or income generating assets. But sadly the Muller land deal became a money-grabbing exercise with temptation to over-look the bigger picture.

Poor leadership The tragedy for Britain is the lack of a governing class brave enough to make big decisions. There was a time when institutions set the boundaries of acceptable behaviour; and for family life it was fundamentally the Church; but disturbingly faith is becoming less significant. Too many facets of our society are getting forever lighter and more out of control, with the growing undertone of aggression making Britain a monstrous and more disturbing place than it was; it is time to build sanity into society and trust into community.

Money-grabbing and debt seems to be what society is all about these days In New Year 2015 the news headlines reported another crisis in the health service, through staff shortages and cut-backs in particular; causing the system to buckle under unprecedented pressure. This contributed to the need for ambulances to queue sometimes for hours before they could unload their sick patients, at one hospital in the north there were eighteen ambulances lined-up waiting at one time. What is the prospect of this dire situation ever improving? It is difficult for us ordinary folk to understand the big political picture, but surely there is something radically wrong in Government. The present Government was elected on its Tory values predominately, couple these with the Christian values that underpin our society, factor in the need for austerity with the economic down-turn, and what do you get? Disaster!

Too much posing and posturing All politicians love posturing, and they would even turn up for the opening of an envelope if there was chance of a picture in a paper. Yet, a far greater priority is to accept that the country cannot afford to carry on as a bloated, high taxing, welfare-heavy nation, without fighting the notion that you can endlessly suck more tax out of businesses and the nation, but with an election coming up we can only expect weak politicians to bribe voters with endless amounts of even more borrowed cash. Surely it is better to keep taxes at reasonable rates and then discipline the country to live within these means. It is perplexing that the Tory government has not shown more competent leadership skills, instaed they are instilling a loss of confidence with far too much posing and posturing, whilst offering little of substance to justify their questionable judgment. This is not the style of leadership required for the moment, particularly during these terribly dangerous and difficult times.

Mrs. Thatcher was revered for being a great leader, she had the moral fibre, the political back-bone and the bulldog spirit to fight for what really mattered. She was brave, resolute and fearless in her pursuit of making the right decisions in the best interest of the country. She was not vain, she did not pamper to personal popularity, and despite having to make unpopular decisions, and not being without her own faults, Mrs. Thatcher showed superb leadership which set this country on the right track for prosperity. Demonstrating sound judgment and remarkable strength of character earned her the title of the greatest twentieth century peacetime Prime Minister.

Strong leadership There has never been a time when the qualities in good leadership have been recognised and appreciated, more than now, and fortunately history reminds us what was achieved by the trio of Regan, Thatcher and Gorbachev. It is times like this that we also reflect back to the days of the Statesmen of stature who led us through those deeply worrying times, Churchill, Truman and Eisenhower, but it is not known if they actually played much golf.

FIFTEEN

Just how many pairs of shoes did Imelda Marcos have?

We expected the Tory Government to be much more assertive Through sensational headlines in early 2015 it was claimed that the Labour Party which had been in power until 2010 knew that the British economy was about to fall off the edge of a cliff a year before it happened in 2008, and that Labour leaders attempted to save their own skins, rather than minimise the impact on the UK economy. However, when a Tory Government came into power, even in coalition, it was never expected that our country would still be in a deep financial predicament nearing the end of their term, with little prospect of the situation changing. It has been so disappointing that tougher stances have not been achieved with expenditure. These are deeply worrying times the debt has reached a stratospheric level, it is inconceivable that the whole country has allowed this to happen. Have the Tory party fulfilled their 2010 election promises, have they heck!

Is the Establishment to blame for the countries moral and economic decline? Our Government's approach to its debt crisis sends the wrong signals to society, uncontrollable debt is shameful, and it represents questionable judgment and poor financial control. No wonder our society has become obsessed with greed and materialism; society has become rotten from the top down through the examples that have been set. Is it time to ask if the 'Establishment' is to blame for the countries moral and economic decline? Who was it that said 'The greatest gift I can give you is the example I have set?'

The Foreign Aid policy This year £13 billion pounds will be spent by our Government on Foreign Aid, which represent 7% of GDP – Gross Domestic Product. This will be sent to twenty eight countries, amongst them Pakistan which is set to receive £310 million, India to receive £250 million (this is despite India having a multi-million pound space programme) and Russia with its billionaire Prime Minister will receive £1.3 million. Interestingly, Imran Khan a political leader in Pakistan, has said that this aid is madness and that much of it is syphoned off by corrupt officials to enrich the lives of a fortunate few, and the bulk never reaches deserving people. Indeed, a report has concluded that aid money did nothing to help the economies and political freedoms of the people in the countries receiving the cash, yet still the Tories give it away whilst turning a blind-eye to the suffering of our own people.

Is this Political madness? It is claimed the UK Government, through its Department for International Development created an ugly rush by distributing £60 million per day, yes, we repeat, giving away £60 million per day during the months of Novemeber –December 2013 in a desperate attempt to meet the Foreign-aid target that had been set. This sort of hasty action leads to people doing stupid things.

To substantiate the Foreign-Aid policy the claim is made that humanity must help the many millions of people suffering under tyrannical regimes, but surely throwing huge amounts of money into the countries is not the wisest approach; dealing with the cause of their problems would be more appropriate; but it would take leaders of great stature to attempt that. How many pairs of shoes did Imelda Marcos have when she and her husband, the tyrannical President of the Philippines, were over-thrown in a coup in 1986, was it 3000? Yes it was!

Financial nightmare For those of us who manage to juggle the household budget quite successfully, it is staggering to comprehend how the Government is going to juggle its own budget. With a Tory Government, even in coalition, it was never expected that our country would still be in a deep financial predicament with little prospect of the situation changing. It has been so disappointing that a tougher stance has not been achieved with Government expenditure. These are deeply worrying times and the debt has reached a stratospheric level, it is inconceivable that the whole country has allowed this to happen

The UK debt stands at a staggering £1.4 trillion With the country having an enormous national debt of £1.4 trillion, this has to be serviced by paying interest, look closer and an even bleaker picture emerges. Presently the Government pays interest of £1 billion per week, yes, every week; and in 2017 this interest requirement is expected to be £70 billion per year. Just to confirm, that is interest only! Where do the Tories get their myth of economic credibility from? Why is the public misled on the state of the country?

During their time in office the Coalition will have added an extra £530 billion to the national debt; that is not all, it really does get worse. To bail out the banks in 2008 the Government borrowed an extra £900 billion, but this figure is excluded from the national debt, to prevent the situation looking too bad. In September 2014 the National debt reached £1.45 trillion, representing 80% GDP and was £100 billion higher than the same point the year before, but the Government still has not grasped a 'good-housekeeping' strategy to reduce it.

At the start of 2015 the deficit, (the difference between inputs and out-puts) is running at a staggering £90 billion a year; with such free spending, how is this deficit ever to be brought under control? Surely a Government's priority is to its own country and particularly in keeping its own citizens safe.

However, back in 2010 the opinion polls gave the Tory party concern there was a prospect they may have just one term in power, and having observed the struggles and compromises the Obama administration faced at their last election, our Tory Government followed the American suit, and directed much attention to appeasing gay marriage and other minority groups as a matter of priority in preparation for the 2015 General Election. During this time rather less focus was on getting to grips with tighter financial control of the bloated welfare budget, not to mention the foreign aid budget.

So Britain is mortgaged to the hilt, and sinking under a mountain of debt whilst our Government leaders portray the country as a 'World power', when the facts paint a darker picture. The situation would be laughable if it were not so serious. There has never been greater need to adopt restraint on expenditure and to focus on rebuilding the nation's infrastructure, defence and economic capacity, as a critical obligation to our national well-being and of course to help revive the country's flagging spirits.

A fine performance Prime Minister As David Cameron was making a most impressive speech to the United Nations Assembly in New York in September 2012, the storm clouds of wroth were already massing around the world. His speech confirmed that fundamentally Cameron is a good man, he means well, but we have to wonder if he is out of his depth, and lacking the stature for troubled times of this magnitude. In fact in different circumstances he would be a superb leader, but the complex problems in our country and in the world today require a leader with enormous strength of character and diplomacy; characteristics that are not evident in any of the leaders of our main parties.

Did the Tory party make dodgy economic claims? After speaking at the Tory Party Conference in October 2014, our Tory Government leaders, were publicly rapped by Sir Anthony Dilnot, Chairman of UK Statistics Authority who found it necessary to point out that for the second year running the they were making false financial claims in what appeared to be a deliberate attempt to mislead the public about the failure to reduce the National debt. Oh dear! Surely not.

So it is disappointing that our Governments leaders do not appear to have lived up to expectation, and that they may be inclined to tell little porkies to defend their precarious economic position; this must make us more guarded and more inclined to scrutinise political claims and policies. The Government's record to date is disappointing as we also notice the frailty of the coalition, the outlook is really rather gloomy, in fact so gloomy that you have to wonder if any party really, really wants to win the next election.

Political vanity! So, how are we to view the credentials of our Government leaders and their spin doctors who appear to be so obsessed with appearance that a re-shuffle was required in the Cabinet simply to make the team look less male, pale and stale for TV cameras? Vanity has no place during troubling times, as Churchill would surely have agreed.

Mixed reports are heard about Vladimir Putin, yet he is emerging as the strongest leader, as he strives for his country to be respected again, he also appears to be the only leader looking after his people, unlike the self-serving leaders that we have here.

How does all this affect us in Shropshire Despite the Government's 'off the scale level of debt' and its precarious financial problem, it has still committed to sending £13 billion in foreign aid, and it can only do this by cutting all public services, and that means the public services in Shropshire too; which will impact each and every one of us. It is inevitable that the establishment will look after itself, and the brunt of austerity will be taken by taxpayers and rural communities. This is why financial cuts have caused another crisis in hospitals over this last Christmas, it is why Shropshire Council is under pressure to cut services, it is why our streets are not cleaned as often as they were, it is why the roads are in poor condition and riddled with pot-holes, it is why after the first snow of 2015 driving conditions are treacherous with roads not having been salted or cleared, it is why we do not have a police presence in Cleobury Mortimer any more, it is why the public transport service is so poor and it is why the youth budget has been cut by 50%.

The questionable Tory example in Shropshire In 2014 it was claimed that the 'UKIP fox was in the Westminster hen house', such was the impact this minor party was having on national politics; and on the disenchanted electorate. As much as we support and admire the stance of UKIP and are pleased at their rise, it is doubtful they would unseat our Ludlow MP. You could pin a Tory rosette on a turd around here and it would get elected; but stranger things have happened; and a sharp drop in the Tory majority might actually concentrate their mind a little! Prior to any general election, the media spotlight is on the opposing parties as they embark on their campaigns of political warfare, with each party out to discredit the others. Now it could be said that South Shropshire is a natural Tory constituency, and that middle class people of a conservative disposition go into politics, but in recent years we have seen Tory Councillors and Tory party members behaving in a manner that suggests they do not always deserve to be in power, having at times set the most appalling examples, by showing a lack of propriety that makes them appear unsuitable for political responsibility. Since we now live in a world where such people refuse to behave honourably, a mechanism needs to be in place to get rid of them from public life.

Where have the Tory gentlemen gone? Anyone thinking of attending a Cleobury Mortimer branch Tory fund-raiser should beware of encountering one or two rather odious men who have a weakness for groping any female in a skirt; these men can also have the audacity to act as if they have a right to grope in such an offensive manner; but fore-warned is fore armed, and provided females are equipped with a suitably chiseled stiletto with which to stand on the offender's foot with one's full weight; and also a suitably positioned knee directed in the groin region of the same perpetrator, it is to be assumed they get the message that groping is not the conduct of honourable Tory gentlemen; besides these men would also benefit from being reminded to have far more respect for our British moral values, which is not a choice or an option, it is a duty; and a responsibility for all those who live in our islands.

Conservatism What the people want is very simple, they want a Government as good as its promises. We all want similar things in life, freedom, the chance for prosperity, to see few people suffering as possible, we want healthy children, to live crime free, the belief in personal responsibility, limited Government, free market, individual liberty, and strong national defence. Conservatism is not so much a philosophy as an attitude, a constant force, performing a timeless function in the development of a free society. However, there is concern that all is not as we would like it to be, that the Tory party has changed its image and its policies, and that Westminster has created an unequal society and an unbalanced economy.

Immigrants demonstrate that they can be woefully misjudged, and that they are also likely to have Tory instincts, because they have had the guts and drive to travel vast distances here to make life better for themselves and their families which all requires a degree of pre-planning. Concerns are becoming prevalent that as society has progressed it has come at a very high price, with each day bringing shocking headlines that suggest that we are in a world more dangerous than ever experienced before; with threats to our liberties becoming ever closer

Where do we live? We appear to live in two Britain's, one containing the silent majority is self-sufficient, intent on maintaining decent standards and doing the right thing; the other which is small, noisy, selfish, intolerant, attention-seeking and destructive; well that's a surprise!

SIXTEEN

'British values were upheld even during war time'.

Celebrating war efforts 2014 was an extraordinary year in so much that it revealed that the world is possibly in a more dangerous state than it has ever been before, but the year also marked the celebrations of Great War efforts.

D day 70 years ago This celebration marked Britain's greatest military exercise ever, when awesome sacrifices were made so that Europe could be free. The invasion of the Normandy beaches could so easily have failed but for the extraordinary tenacity and courage off the men who fought on June 6th 1944. Heroes were sent to combat by Churchill and Roosevelt, an alliance that made victory possible. The world remembers, but what if anything has been learned? As memory fades into history, new tensions now cast their shadows as we are faced with the link between sacrifices of 1944 and the menaces of 2014.

Poppies From July – Nov 11 2014 a sea of ceramic poppies created a spectacular display that encircled the iconic landmark, the Tower of London. Over 880,000 ceramic poppies were created to form a powerful visual commendation for the First World War centenary, the scale of the instillation was intended to reflect the magnitude of such an important centenary. Each poppy represented a British military fatality. The First World War was the conflict supposed to end all wars, yet despite the pious hope, the summer of 2014 was also a time of mayhem, slaughter and terrifying instability, with victims begging for intervention. When future historians look back it is likely that the year will be seen as a watershed moment marking the end of the cold war. So how tragic to see our Armed forces sliced and diced and mutilated when the outlook for peace is so clouded and uncertain; it is deeply disturbing to observe the reduction on the nation's defence to less than 2% of overall budget, whilst the foreign-aid budget is increased, a political decision that beggars belief.

British values upheld even during war time Even during the ravages of war years civility was undiminished, as was kindness and respect, everyone was equally civil and courteous in return. Since then something insidiously nasty has eroded that erstwhile unbreakable pride. The values and attitudes of our rich and civilised society have been whittled away by moronically blinkered liberal do-gooders who seem to hate our English culture as much as the Islamic terrorists do.

The rot probably started in the sixties when youth began debunking authority in the name of freedom. Once a child refuses to recognise authority then the future can mean only an inability to instill any authority in the generations to come. The vicious cycle extends and permeates to all members of society.

English culture There was a time when English culture was once the yard-stick by which the civilised societies of the world were measured. But social media has given a platform to bullies and rogues to propagate an unsavoury influence, but society must not succumb to negative change, it must assert to clean up its act, fix its social problems and reassert its traditional values. After all a lack of manners and respect can only be a reflection of what a community thinks of itself, like the tragic deterioration of civilised behavior as reflected by acts of drunkenly kicking cars and screaming insults. The traditional virtues of male chivalry and female propriety are too often very far from view.

How did it happen How did we move from a civilised society to a position where we are fearful of the threat posed by a dominant group so violent and extreme. The troubles in the Middle East are now impacting on our civil liberties and everything our English culture represents. It is claimed that one hundred Mercedes cars were sent to journalists in the Middle East, but what would the purpose be, other than attempt to influence the media reporting on these toxic cultural influences, one way or another, but it also does much to emphasise the power of propaganda. Is it time to ask if civilisation has gone far enough, and is the degeneration of society what happens at the end of empires.

Trojan horse It is claimed that twenty years ago the Government was first informed by a Cleric; about his concerns that Islam was making strides into British education, but the matter was not taken seriously until now; in fact behind the Trojan Horse scandal are issues symptomatic of far wider concerns. In the wake of the Trojan horse scandal emerging in Birmingham in 2014, where it was discovered education was being infiltrated to brainwash the young, it became clear that the fear of Islam advancing its threat to undermine our national values was increasing. However, the Government has responded by giving reassurance with its plans to actively promote our British values; stating that these values are not an option they are vital.

The world has become a dangerous place, not because of those who do evil things, but because of those who look on and do nothing. The belief in freedom, tolerance, accepting personal and social responsibility, respecting and upholding the law are things we should try and live by every day and we need to be far more assertive about promoting these values, and the institutions that uphold them. In recent years society became lax and this has led to divisions and allowed extremism to flourish, already Jihadists are controlling thousands of minds through social media. A high price is being paid for taking the biblical standards of righteousness out of state schools. As Greek philosopher Aristotle said: 'No notice is taken of little evil, but when it increases it strikes the eye'.

Be more relevant in society Society has reached a tipping point and no community can carry on in this manner; it is time to look at the measures needed to build a trusting community and a trusting society. There has never been a greater need to become more relevant to society, to take an interest in matters beyond local gossip. Gossiping is a fruitless exercise it serves only to entertain and stimulate; but being proactive would serve a more useful purpose. It is the influence of each and every one of us to help shape societies and communities, in doing so it is important to keep spirits up. Sometimes it is best avoiding people or pastimes that bring us down; instead the need is to seek to reinforce thoughtfulness towards others, kindness in the community, honesty in business and fairness in all things.

Good qualities in society When learning about the qualities that make a good society, it is wise to acknowledge the strong emphasis on values and development of character, which involve the teaching of the difference between good and bad, the importance of punctuality, respect for others, and the need for kindness and consideration. Underpinning a good society is the character building achieved through education. Schools attempt to ensure it is truly understood that self-discipline is required in the world of work, whether you feel like going to work or not.

It is a daunting challenge Restoring a fractured society is a daunting challenge, but not an invincible one; as long as the courage and fortitude is ready, and the ability to summon up the political will to defend our values and way of life with the same determination, courage and tenacity with which we have faced danger before in our history, then it can be achieved. Then there is also the need to encourage people to stop and think about issues that they have never considered before. There remains no choice but to rise to the challenge and to re-build a good society – with the need to be more forthright in commending what is right and condemning what is wrong. There is need to strive for peace and harmony, and to work within a spirit of co-operation, and to endeavour to help others whenever we can.

SEVENTEEN

As Greek philosopher Aristotle - 'No notice is taken of little evil, but when it increases it strikes the eye'.

Mumfords @ war After mentioning the commemorative war efforts earlier, it reminds us that currently Mumfords remains at cold war with our local Cleobury Parish Council. In recognition of the Royal Wedding in 2010 the Parish Council purchased a quantity of commemorative mugs to give to each child within the community. There were about 169 mugs left over, and at Mumfords we agreed to try to sell them on behalf of the Council. However, during the time the process was underway a change in circumstances occurred, with the town's administration bringing the town into disrepute by manipulating and falsifying public records. This was followed by the brazen and audacious move to publish the falsified minutes openly on-line.

When Mumfords received a letter regarding the outstanding mugs, the response from Mumfords was that outstanding monies and mugs would not be returned to the Council until all falsified minutes had been corrected. Needless to say, it could be claimed that Mumfords should not be with holding public money, but equally so, it should be claimed that it is unlawful for any public servant to produce falsified records. So we are in stale-mate, a catch twenty-two situation, but make no mistake, Mumfords will certainly be not be accommodating the demands of any dodgy civic representatives. The primary point is not to nail a nasty, but to stop whatever dodgy antics they are up to.

It happened over-night In 2012 Cleobury Mortimer Parish Council went from being a fair and balanced administration, into one that was blighted by a toxic combination of questionable credentials, and even more questionable conduct, and it happened literally over-night. At the core is the conduct of civic representatives that have at times behaved like shady sleazebags, having immersed themselves into the corrupt atmosphere of the day, and there is no question the town deserves much better. It is a civic responsibility to ensure the accuracy and the propriety of everything that local administration represents. Suggestions that some may have submitted inaccurate CV's, might go some way to explain why in office some have struggled with the ability to produce anything that is accurate.

Beware The door of the local administration office should have a 'Beware' notice; It is from there, that there has been a failure to comply with recognised good legal practice; it is also from there that the skill of manipulating official details has turned local politics into a mindless cynical circus by coercing others into the same malpractice. This sort of behavior cannot be countenanced and taking full account of the important principle of proportionality, the interests of the public far outweigh the interests of any such questionable civic practice.

Community Led Plan During July 2014 Cleobury Mortimer Parish Council produced a 'Community Led Plan' which had the intended purpose of collating data from the community, and processing it to produce a reliable document. In fact it has been the obligation of every parish to produce such a plan as a useful reference guide. Whilst containing some useful information, the Cleobury plan emerged as a distorted and misleading account of life in this part of South Shropshire, and cannot go uncorrected. It is quite wrong to portray this community to be a rural idyll when at its heart are such deep-rooted problems that must be booted out. A community cannot prosper until it has dealt with problems in its past. Disturbingly the data has been collated from response from just 26% of the population which makes the data captured statistically unreliable. It also reflects an apathetic community. (By contrast the CLP for Neen Savage Parish was superbly managed and achieved a response of 63%, offering a strong foundation on which to plan for the future of the parish).

Not much to report then The most curious thing about the Cleobury Community Led Plan report, which was a booklet distributed to every household, was the size of it, it was so small and with limited content. Though details in the Community Led Plan did confirm that in recent generations, higher achievers and those pursuing further education leave Cleobury Mortimer and then seek employment and housing opportunities, elsewhere; which has the impact of leaving a very small pool from which to emerge the future natural leadership of our town. Cleobury Mortimer Community Led Plan – very disappointing, those responsible could have done much better!

Bullies In 2011 Roy Leigh purchased the Old Library, the semi-detached building to the left of the Parish Hall with the intention of using it for a commercial enterprise. During the purchase process, property searches produced nothing untoward. However, it later transpired that a disabled access door had been installed in the Parish Hall without the necessary planning permission for a listed building. This was an error of Shropshire Council planning who did not follow correct procedures, and the problem created an issue of access over the property, which has caused enormous problems, and affected the plans that Roy had for the property. However, Roy and his family have been deeply affected by the fall-out of this controversy that came from no-where, he has been hounded, and faced with a barrage of intimidation and harassment from the Parish Council, which was engineered and executed by civic representatives who had the audacity to publish malicious and defamatory claims against Roy, online, through Council minutes. Roy has installed CCTV cameras, and several images of the troublesome perpetrators on his property are clearly seen.

Civic representatives have behaved appallingly in this matter, through the brazen intimidation of this local resident, but then there is little Civic concern in this town for anyone. The controlling administrative group will be remembered for its opportunistic, negative and bullying image that tarnished the reputation of Cleobury Mortimer even further.

Off to seek better opportunities Down the generations it has been observed that young people go off to University, and those that successfully graduate are inclined to seek better opportunities in more affluent communities particularly with the attraction to gravitate to the cultural advantages offered by the south east, this leaves our town with a concentration of those less ambitious, and with less ability. Hence, the absence of natural leadership, and the inclination of those remaining to think responsibility belongs to others.

Housing Recent housing development has not always helped Cleobury Mortimer, and sometimes the impact has been detrimental. When planning for housing has been applied for, and applications have been submitted for appropriate development; Shropshire council has frequently intervened to influence the provision of a higher ratio of social housing. Too much social housing can be detrimental to any community; yet, even when our local Council has tried to insist on some influence over the allocation of this housing, they have been over-ruled in favor of independent allocators. Thus it can be argued that Cleobury Mortimer has been engineered to become a dumping ground for problem families from a wide area that includes Ludlow, Kidderminster and as far as Wolverhampton. Whilst these families need the opportunity to lead good and well-adjusted lives, the problem is exacerbated within a small town with enough social problems of its own.

A sign of the times At the local primary school a supply of cereals and milk, also a brush and comb, are kept to help the children who are sent to school undernourished and unkempt, what does this say about declining standards in any society?

Domestic violence Families comes in all shapes and sizes, and rare are those that do not have problems at some stage. Police are called out to more incidents of domestic abuse than any other crime in Cleobury Mortimer, to the extent that pregnant women attending ante-natal appointments now find themselves quizzed about their domestic circumstances and are given opportunity to indicate if there is hint of domestic abuse. Many years ago a young local mother left her home and family after she was subjected to domestic abuse that included rape by her father-in-law. However, as she attempted to secure custody of her children she sought local support, the response from neighboring farmers was 'Can't do that, can't turn on a neighbour, what would the consequences be'. Indeed, what would the consequences be! Without collective condemnation of the plight she endured, that young mother had no choice but to go back to the family where she still remains. This case shows how turning a blind eye and a cover-up culture is shamefully endemic even in our own community, and it is the vulnerable who always suffer the most.

Young egos bloated by social media Despite the nation's shaky economic position, youngsters still believe a life of glamour and opportunity will miraculously materialise for them, as social media continues to edit out reality to convey an enviable lifestyle. This notion has already led to a rise in depression rates due to failed expectations. We are in a society that portrays an image that 'greed is good', and that social aspirations, and materialism matter more than anything else. The desire to acquire material things has created a warped society, and the notion 'keeping up with the Jones's has reached epic proportion. Greed blinds against all else particularly that folly can be exposed in showy displays. Wherever we go we are faced with seductive marketing campaigns aimed at influencing a desire in everyone to strive for material success; but an obsession for possessions distracts from the very things that matter most in life, the things that money cannot buy. Society needs to change its attitude, and convey that it is possible to be content with less; as so much harm is caused to a society through over-exposure to marketing that promotes the desire to live beyond one's means, that eventually triggers the risk of getting deeper into debt than ever.

EIGHTEEN

'Consumerism is defined as acquiring things you do not want, with money you do not have to impress people you do not like'.

Educated into debt Not everyone is fortunate, and for many the goal is to look prosperous even if they are deep in debt. The stigma of borrowing was removed many years ago, and people were actually encouraged to borrow, driving us into a nation of debt, without educating young people to understand when it is good and when it is bad. Politicians should hang their heads in shame, it is a Government enforced debt that has been a terrible thing for society, because nobody took custodial care. Youngsters have been educated to accept that debt is the norm without being taught how the competitive consumer economy works. Why pay more for something than you need to? The whole message is about value, do not over pay for things on principle, and help avoid the risk of financial incontinence.

Learning to cook properly Simultaneous to the removal of the debt stigma came the introduction of trendy teaching practices, thus removing from the curriculum activities like cross-country, a sport that requires no fancy facilities and no expensive gear. Also removed was 'home economics', which as its name suggests was all about efficiency in everyday life. A senior politician was recently lambasted in the press, and forced to apologise for making the comment that 'poor people could not cook properly'. She should not have apologised, but she should have amended her comment to say that 'few people can cook well on a budget'. Home economics in schools taught the basic principles of cooking to all pupils, mainly the ability to produce nourishing and nutritious meals at little cost. Of course the skill is to combine cheaper cuts of meat with seasonal vegetables which are always better value, and produce enough to provide a hearty meal for all the family. No fancy recipe books or fancy ingredients are needed, it is just old-fashioned cooking and it works very well.

Parental discipline What kind of parents would we be if we did not set down strict rules? The unpopularity of any decisions must not be an excuse for inaction. When young people move beyond their parental sphere of influence, they can easily be drawn into a culture of relaxed social attitudes that move the focus towards self-interest and self-promotion, which can manifest into an incredible lack of respect and poor attitude that can in turn become beset by discipline issues; and despite the ground rules this can still escalate into full-blown rebellion.

Firm guidelines are required Parents must not be deterred and must remain resolute with the rules and guide lines they have established. It is often feared that in many of the designer prams of today lie some of the over-indulged super-brats of tomorrow. There is a danger of over-nurtured children becoming adults who will never need to try, who will not be geared up to cope with the inevitable challenges that life throws at them. Nothing worthwhile in life can be achieved without discipline, obedience to authority, and hard work. Discipline is learned at home and carried out at school; ensuring that youngsters can flourish where there is structure and order. For society to be well-ordered it is dependent on self-control and intrinsic good behaviour.

English numeracy and literacy – nothing short of a national scandal British schools have plummeted down World Education League Tables leaving them trailing behind Poland, Albania and Estonia, this result is attributed to a poor grasp of literacy and numeracy. The Education Minister said 'The report under-lines the urgent need to reform our school system. We need to learn from best performing schools. Too right we do! This result should be another wake-up call for the Government, who seem unable to read the 'writing on the wall'. Just what is going on in the education system, such inadequacy will result in economic and social problems in the future, as well as wasting the talent of so many young people.

The Far East Nations top the poll Topping the league tables were the Far East nations where their standards appear to be surging ahead, and where their culture prizes effort above ability. This different style of education has been referred to as a demanding tiger-mother approach, where it assumes all children not just the elite few, will work hard, behave well and succeed. It is claimed that they are more inclined to do well if higher expectations are set, and where an atmosphere is created where they are well behaved, calm and respectful; and where negative behavior is frowned upon.

Perseverance and hard-work essential It is also claimed that the importance of perseverance and hard-work can compensate for lack of natural ability, with the need to pair effort with compassion. This shows the advantage of adopting a mind-set that the harder you work the better you will do, and that the increased effort will develop the capacity to learn when combined with ability, particularly if the focus is on subjects of interest. This helps affirm that humility and hard-work are still the key requirement for achieving goals, particularly when combined with self-control, discipline and resilience. While this Far Eastern system has been hailed as an approach that other countries can no longer ignore, many of us would recognise it simply as 'good old fashioned teaching principles'.

What can be learned from Independent schools? A recent report suggested that children in state schools were no longer concerned about winning or losing in sport, and that certain conditions triggered this condition, what a sad indictment this is for society? This report came after our Prime Minister expressed concern that at the 2012 Olympics in London the podiums had been dominated by privately educated athletes. However, does this explain why Independent schools are such a success, with foreign pupils flocking to Britain's boarding schools from countries like Russia, China and Africa. Winning is in the Independent schools DNA, but the need remains, to make sure that pupils also learn to lose with good grace; however, there would be a failing in duty it were not suggested that winning was also important. It is claimed that Independent schools are more successful at teaching character and encouraging success, emphasising that attitude over aptitude should prevail in everything. Whilst this reference is made to sport, the same criteria is relevant to succeeding in modern life where so many aspects are competitive, even trying for one's first job for example.

The consequence of poor education In the twenty first century it is morally wrong that any pupil should leave school after eleven years of education that at times has been so sub-standard, that a pupil can become disaffected when faced with poor employment prospects. But this has occurred in Cleobury Mortimer, where young people have been known to encounter a range of problems if they have left Lacon Childe School at sixteen with no meaningful qualifications. They had probably expected their willingness to graft would open endless opportunities; however, harsh reality soon kicks in. With those unable to afford to learn to drive, they are immediately limited to where they can work; and with Health and Safety regulations imposed at places like most building sites, the notion of even casual work is not easy to find.

The need to vent out despair and frustration Far too often we have witnessed these youngsters venting out the despair of their situation, with the stained glass windows of the Church becoming a prime target for kicking in; indicating this is a cry for help, malice is not really the intention. Young people who find themselves disadvantaged, or maybe discover that society is not as compassionate as they assumed, can easily be drawn to act in a manner that is extreme. There are many young people who deserve extra support and just a bit of encouragement to help them on their way in this self-centred and increasingly competitive society that we live in. Special thanks to St. Mary's Youth Team and all they do.

The Jubilee Centre of Character and Values This facility opened in Birmingham in May 2012, it is a multi-million pound investment funded by a charitable foundation. The aim is to promote and strengthen character within society, within families, with communities and within the work-place. The initiative was established in the wake of the inner city riots of 2011, which were believed to have been triggered by the breakdown of fundamental values in society, this in turn triggered a renewal call for common values and ethical teaching, and a return to 'old fashioned values'. The claim is that character strengths are taught and that they become critical to a life well led, and will benefit all aspects of society if they are more widely in existence. Politicians have failed to provide principled leadership that the country so badly needs; religious leaders have their own problems, and far too often are more intent on disagreeing with each other; and for many people, family life is unfortunately fractured. The Jubilee Centre hopes to help fix Britain's character flaws by promoting the strengths of self-restraint, hard-work, resilience, optimism, courage, generosity, modesty, empathy, kindness and good manners.

The need for the right priorities League tables put pressure on education to produce results, which in turn puts pressure on schools to excel; with the consequence that emphasis on promoting character is lost. With the increase in fractured families, the Government has a greater responsibility to encourage moral values through education, with the need to promote good manners, honesty and punctuality through mainstream curriculum in all schools, together with responsibility, courage, kindness and other virtues. By building character the class divide is closed, and people become happier and more contented.

Young people learn much less from what adults say, than from what they see them doing. It is hoped that by encouraging a stronger grounding of ethics and values within families and schools, coupled with a better example from Political and Church leaders, combined with a more responsible media approach this will help restore the linchpin that creates a well-adjusted society.

Winston Churchill said 'Success is not final, failure is not fatal, it is the courage to continue that counts.'

A strong work ethic This is another old-fashioned virtue that would be useful for many young people today. Those leaving school with few prospects could be helped if they were encouraged to develop a strong work ethic, and when employment is scarce, opportunities can still be abound if one looks hard enough, it is a case of persevering until the right opportunity pops up. In the meantime, there is need for encouragement to find a job, any job, to stay in work and never rely on benefits, by doing so they become employable, it does not matter what the work is, but by working they learn new things, meet new people and they are exposed to new ideas, and they must never underestimate the power of flattery, it puts them in people's minds.

Nurture an attitude Young people need to learn to be helpful, enthusiastic, reliable, dependable, and to make a positive influence which it will put them leaps ahead for the job they really want, because a strong work ethic will be recognised, and it is a strong work ethic which leads to success. It is all about forging the right attitude, and it is also important to point out that devoting energies towards work helps family and society at large. By sharp contrast those fortunate enough to benefit from a trust fund can find that it can become like an albatross round their neck; people who are not required to earn their own money can often be ruined, simply by lacking aspiration or any particular focus.

What on earth is happening in education? It is through schools and through education that impressionable young people are influenced most. Whilst the Government policy in education is working better, there is need to question leadership and those that teach in schools. There seems to be an alarming number of cases reported of inappropriate relationships between teachers and pupils in state schools, it is a matter that needs addressing with a sense of urgency, doing nothing is not an option, and any wishy-washy approach will be out of touch with public opinion. The matter needs to be put into context, with the horror felt by the revelation of the scale of cases of abuse, that have taken place predominantly in Catholic boarding schools across the land, the results are shaming for everyone involved in running these schools. It is obviously a closed world for the matter to have remained concealed for so long; it further adds to the claim that abuse starts at the top, with Eton included in the list of top schools that are affected.

Buddhist quote: 'However many holy words you read, however many you speak, what good will they do if you do not act upon them'.

Sometimes we are baffled Sometimes we can be baffled by the conduct of the Church, particularly when their actions defy what they represent. Abuse cases have soared and the Catholic Church has been tainted by the scandals; the Pope de-frocked nearly 400 priests during 2011-12, with Pope Benedict adding that he was mortified by the scale of the child abuse and simply did not understand 'how priests could fail in such a way'. It has even been suggested that Pope Benedict's decision to retire could have been influenced by the scale of moral decline he became mindful of, even at the Vatican.

The Anglican Church has similarly been affected with abuse charges brought against high profile Clerics; with the Archbishop of Canterbury saying that he feared more bad stories could emerge. Experts believe recent growing awareness of such offences has helped victims come forward, and the culture of emotional restraint which meant many victims suffered in silence is now outdated. Again it comes down to weak leadership, and those who may not have been assertive enough in condemning malpractice, when it first emerged. Decadence has taken on a mind of its own.

A local problem A slightly similar problem arose at a school in Cleobury Mortimer recently, which involved a teacher whose conduct was not deemed appropriate for the profession or status. However, despite the concerns it was with great difficulty that this matter was brought to the attention of Shropshire Council; whilst this matter is now resolved, and the person has left the position; it must be recognised that without members of this community brave enough to persist with the matter, there would have been no response to the complaints and another cover-up policy would have been implemented.

NINETEEN

'Too many prefer their play-boy lifestyles rather than giving any consideration or obligation to social responsibility'.

Neen Savage Parish needs help with a problem Just what do you do with an errant publication? So often angst is aroused when a very rich vein of discontent is tapped into, and in this case it is the use or misuse of the parish magazine. The Vital Link is the main form of communication within the community of only about three hundred residents, and it is generally a newsy publication. However, the editors rather naughtily are using the publication in a manipulative way, putting it rather bluntly they have turned it into another propaganda rag. It has also been understandable that suggestions have arisen that the Vital Link could possibly be under fascist influence, but it is certainly hope that is not the case.

Neen Savage Parish Council contributes to the cost of this publication, yet is unable to benefit from balanced or favourable news coverage. The issue printed in December 2014 contained details of three Council meetings with the report having been written by the Vital Link editors. It is noted that the report is not balanced or accurate, and has been written in a manner as to undermine the Council, and to mislead the electorate, confirming that the Vital Link in no longer a reliable publication. So high time to raise the journalistic standards there.

People are influenced by the conduct of those around them When those in public life or in positions of responsibility behave inappropriately, what sort of message does that send out to the community? It is claimed that people are influenced more by what they see others do, rather than what others say. When this involves Civic leaders and members of our Churches, it is understandable that this has a deep and profound impact. In Cleobury Mortimer and Neen Savage we have had to bear witness to some of those in positions of influence being corrupt, dishonest, deceitful, tyrannical and financially reckless; there is need to consider how this conduct reflects on community and young people in particular?

At a Council meeting in Neen Savage in the autumn of 2014 which was called to discuss a planning application, the Clerk was explaining that he been unable to arrange a site meeting for the complex application because there was a lack of co-operation with the applicant; when the applicant suddenly piped up from the public seats, and made a derogative comment before adding that he did not intend to permit the Council on his property! Curiously this same person had made a comment on an earlier occasion when he claimed that his company used 'gold watches' to always get what they want. Dare we ask if anyone in local Government has a gold watch? That is not in any way making an assertion, it is merely seeking clarity on the assurance given by the Home Secretary Theresa May that transparency and accountability would take precedence in public life, and it is not known that she was excluding Shropshire Council from that directive.

Setting examples for society What can be done to help a society beset with such a range of complex problems? Why not begin by raising awareness? Why not also, always focus on the positive?

Farmers Markets The introduction of the monthly Farmers Markets to our town by Cleobury Country Ltd. must be the most significant initiative to help prosperity and social cohesion; prominently sited in and around St. Mary's Church, the market with its striking and colourful range of flags brings a touch of excitement and anticipation. Claire and her team have done a marvellous job bringing the traders and everything together; if only Claire with her friendly and sunny disposition had been at the helm of our town years ago, our problems would never have arisen.

Where do we go from here? Without major change, public confidence in the way our community is run, will soon collapse altogether. We turn to leaders for wisdom, reassurance and decisions, and we need leadership – not dithering, posturing and waffle. The underlying principle should be the responsibility in life to contribute with compassion, understanding, and respect for others, to be part of a forging community which cannot fail to influence and attract others striving for a better society, the task is big. Cleobury Mortimer needs a Council that will command public confidence and will earn public trust, and what we have at the moment does not do that; this town should be supportive of whatever it takes to restore public credibility. Awareness must come to the fore when any future leadership of this town is considered, the electorate must be cautious when approving anyone seeking a position in public life, and it will be imperative that credentials are closely examined, and if possible the implementation of psychopathic screening.

Tesco During 2014 the mighty Tesco found itself in a sticky situation with problems in the company likely to cause embarrassment, so it decided to come clean. A new Chief Executive was appointed, then the decision was taken to revert the company back to its true values in an attempt to restore its battered reputation and to rebuild trust. A commendable course of action that will earn Tesco much respect.

Set the standards high! Why not set our own public standards high, and look at the qualities of great leaders, and aspire to ensure our town is led by those of similar calibre. Mandela with his tough, pragmatic and principled stance immediately comes to mind; Churchill inspired with his moral stature. It is about being an advocate of popular democracy, of being principled, having good judgment and integrity, having a generous spirit, being humble and appreciative, and having entered politics for all the right reasons. People thrive in well-functioning communities, and only through good leadership can Cleobury Mortimer become a well-functioning community that strives to be prosperous, vibrant and cohesive

Leadership guidelines The 'Josephson Institute of Ethics' offers a list of recommendations that when put into a political context aims to focus the energy of people into striving to make society more honest, fair, caring and accountable.

- **Trustworthiness** - This is dependent on the core values of honesty, integrity, reliability and loyalty; and is the most fundamental ethical value, having a broader concept than many realise; it includes communicating in a way unlikely to mislead or deceive, avoiding sloppy judgement. Sincerity is to be genuine and to preclude all acts that lead to false or misleading impressions.

- **Honesty in conduct** - This is about playing fair, without cheating, fraud, subterfuge or trickery. Cheating is a particularly foul form of dishonesty, as it seeks to take advantage of those who are not cheating; a violation of both trust and fairness.
- **Integrity** - This is the consistency between words acts and beliefs.
- **Reliability** - The commitment that creates a legitimate basis for others to depend on.
- **Loyalty** - Loyalty is a responsibility to promote public interests
- **Respect** - The Golden Rule – 'Do unto others as you would have them do unto you', illustrates the pillar of respect. Respect prohibits humiliation, manipulation and exploitation, but reflects notions such as civility, courtesy, decency, dignity, autonomy, tolerance and acceptance. A respectful person is an attentive listener, one who treats others with consideration, and never resorts to intimidation or coercion.
- **Responsibility** - This is shown by being accountable, pursuing excellence through a moral obligation to do one's best whilst exercising self-restraint.
- **Perseverance** - Responsible people finish what they start, overcoming rather than surrendering to obstacles. Always striving to improve.
- **Self-restraint** - The need to exercise self-control.
- **Fairness** - Involving issues of equality, impartiality and openness. Impartiality without prejudice.
- **Caring** - Caring is at the heart of ethics, and ethical decision making, and the good relations with others.
- **Citizenship** - This includes the civic virtues and duties that advise behaviour within community; doing ones best to make society work, now and for future generations, with the need to inspire community to feel passionate

Lack of leadership Standing on our shop steps at Mumfords, glancing up and down the street, the outlook looks rather grim. When the prosperity and stability of our town depends on good leadership, and having established the credentials that are required in any future candidates, where is the pool of talent that future leaders are going to emerge from, none can be seen?

Playboy lifestyle Most people do not give a monkeys about politics, and besides, there is no general desire to devote time to any public life these days, and who can blame anyone. But if everyone adopted the same stance, where would we be? Then of course, for many there is the apathy towards work, with several generations of uninterrupted prosperity having created an apathetic approach to anything inconvenient and requiring effort; thus many minds are not ready to cope with the battle against political corruption and an unstable society. Maybe it is time to temper this outlook with a stiff dose of reality! There are still many within the land-owning and business community with the ability, but they have had it far too easy, and the prospect of committing themselves to any element of social responsibility could not be contemplated if it were likely to interfere with their playboy life-styles!

TWENTY

Inspiration and a ray of hope . . . . .

An **indelible good** Despite the problems listed in this book there is still an indelible amount of good within our community, though it may be difficult to see at times; and there are still many good and decent people with small voices striving to do their very best for lots of aspects of community life. May the influence of these people flourish and become prominent, quashing all the destructive influences of the past.

It is New Year 2015 - A ray of hope at the end of the street At the far end of our street lives a young man who has already shown an interest in public life, and at the election in 2013 Jack Martin became a member of Cleobury Mortimer Parish Council when he was only eighteen years old. Jack's interest in local politics followed a pattern he had already set for having an interest and concern for many aspects of our community. Jack is very much involved in the Cleobury Brass Band, he is an accomplished player and teaches others; heads have been turned by this performer. That apart, Jack has exceptional credentials, he had been Headboy at Lacon Childe School and he lives in what was the back-yard of his great-grandfathers building business which was based at what was the old Redfern Hotel, opposite the Old Lion.

Jack lives next door to his grandfather Tom Webb who still works in the building trade. Both Jack and his mother are talented with brass instruments, they acquired their musical gifts from Tom. Tom Webb's family came from nearby Parish of Hopton Bank which is on the way to Clee Hill, where his grandfather, an accomplished musician established a brass band in which he played with his six sons. Subsequently this band moved its base to Cleobury Mortimer and Tom eventually became its linchpin; and now much of the responsibility for Cleobury Brass Band has passed to Jack.

Sir Winston Churchill This man is hailed as the greatest Englishman and our greatest Prime Minister; Churchill served during 1940-45 and then from 1951-55, and his life has been unparalleled in time. It is for the impact of his speeches that he is now justly remembered. Churchill sought to drive and enthuse those around him, and his ability to lift the spirits of the British people in times of adversity was neatly balanced with a sparkling line of withering put-downs.

Demonstrating extraordinary leadership, he was bold, brave and tireless in his resolve to take on the might of Nazi Germany, he inspired a nervous and hesitant Britain through his sheer energy and force of personality to defy stark odds and never to give in. The entire world's history would have been different if Churchill had not come to power in Britain in 1942. Sensible people see the magnitude of what he achieved, his legacy is everywhere in the modern world.

Churchill 2015 - January 2015 saw the commemoration of the fiftieth anniversary of the death of Sir Winston Leonard Spencer-Churchill in 1965, and seventy-five years since his finest hour on becoming our wartime Prime Minister. This was a unique International Celebration of the life and legacy of Sir Winston Churchill, commemorated to keep his memory alive as well as educate and inspire future generations.

Some of Churchill's quotes:

- This is the lesson: 'Never give in, never give in, never, never, never, never, in nothing, great or small, large or petty, never give in except to conviction of honour and good sense'.
- Never yield to force, never yield to the apparently over-whelming might of the enemy'.
- 'All great things are simple and many can be expressed in a simple word – freedom, justice, honour, duty, mercy, hope'.
- 'Never, ever, ever, ever, give up'.
- 'It is a fine thing to be honest, but it is also important to be right'.
- 'The farther back you look, the farther forward you are likely to see'.

- 'You have enemies? Good that means you have stood up for something, sometime in your life'.
- 'Courage is what it takes to stand up and speak, courage is also what it takes to sit down and listen'.
- 'The pessimist sees the difficulty in every situation, the optimist sees the opportunity in every difficulty'.
- 'No boy or girl should ever be disheartened by lack of success in their youth, but should diligently and faithfully continue to persevere and make up for lost time'.
- 'Many men stumble across the truth - but most manage to pick themselves up and continue as if nothing happened'.
- 'Attitude is a little thing that can make a big difference'.
- 'If you are going through hell, keep going'.
- 'How much easier it is to join bad companions than to shake them off'. 1943
- 'Always be guarded against tyranny, whatever shape it may assume'
- 'I am not a pillar of the Church, but a buttress, I support it from the outside' 1954

<u>Other inspirational quotes</u>:

Stalin on politics The people who cast the votes decide nothing, while the people who count the votes decide everything.

Peter T. McIntyre Confidence comes from not always being right, but from not fearing to be wrong.

Charles Darwin It is not the strongest of species that survive, nor the most intelligent, but the one most responsive to change.

Bishop of Hereford Today the world produces enough food to feed all seven billion of its inhabitants, so why is it that still nearly one billion go without?

Japanese proverb One kind word can warm three winter month

TWENTY ONE

George Orwell on the dangers facing the
modern world - 'Don't let it happen'.

George Orwell This was the pen name of Eric Arthur Blair 1903 – 1950.
He was an English writer noted for his critical thoughts, and his views on
culture and social injustice; he went on to be ranked amongst the most
influential writers of the twentieth Century. His book '1984' was written in
1948 by and is widely read as social comment and even a chilling prophecy.
While 1984 has come and gone, Orwell's narrative is as timeless as ever, he
presents a startling and haunting vision that is so powerful it is convincing
from start to finish.

He claimed that 'war against a foreign country only happens when the
affluent classes think they are going to profit from it'; adding that 'in our
age there is no such thing as keeping out of politics. All issues are political
issues, and politics itself can be a mass of lies, evasions, folly, hatred and
schizophrenia'. 'If liberty means anything at all, it means the right to tell
people what they do not want to hear'. He is quoted 'In a time of universal
deceit telling the truth is a revolutionary act'.

'Don't let it happen' Orwell's prophetic final words on the madness
of the modern world. The parody is that something like 1984 could
actually happen. The author envisaged the future as dark and terrifying,
as he observed the direction the world was going in at that time, claiming
that 'In our world there will be no emotions except fear, rage, triumph
and self-abasement. There will be no loyalty, but there will always be the
intoxication of power, always at every moment there will be the thrill of
victory, the sensation of trampling on the enemy who is helpless; if you
want a picture of the future, imagine a boot stamping on a human face
forever. The moral to be drawn from this dangerous nightmare situation,
is a simple one, don't let it happen'.

TWENTY TWO

As Gandhi said - 'Be the change you want to see'.

Buddhism – **Thought provoking and relevant** Maybe the time has come to give some consideration to the message portrayed by the Dalai Lama, who through his wisdom, honesty and humour urges people to take action to make the world a better and more peaceful place through service and non-violence. His Holiness the Dalai Lama has emerged as an International Statesman for peace as he highlights the importance of developing compassion and kindness using uplifting and wise words.

The importance of whole-heartedness The Dalai Lama emphasises that most people strive for happiness, contentment and peace of mind; but these things cannot come without warm-heartedness, which in itself reduces ill-feeling and distrust; he adds that society is now influenced by whatever advertising and the media portrays through popular TV and sports channels; but no-where or by no-one is warm-heartedness encouraged or taught. Society must emphasise much more strongly that if you do wrong things there are negative consequences.

A way of life Buddhism is recognised as a way of life with a code of practice that has become increasingly popular in western countries for a number of reasons; the philosophy seems to have answers to many of the problems in modern materialistic society and also the deep understanding the faith has of the human mind, which is now recognised and accepted by prominent psychologists as being both advanced and effective.

The dangers caused by a materialistically orientated culture are that it cannot last, it always leads to deep economic and social problems. But if a society were to change, to focus instead on its general well-being, by encouraging people to lead happier lives, it would develop the satisfaction that comes from peace of mind; and despite some people having difficult lives it is still possible to achieve the calm and contentment that comes from peace of mind. A contented society becomes friendly, kind and caring.

Buddhism The claim by Buddhism is that 'We have no need for temples, no need for complicated philosophy; our own minds and our own hearts are our temples, and kindness is our philosophy'.

Gandhi quotes:

- 'Happiness is when, what you think, what you say and what you do are in harmony'.
- 'The best way to find yourself is to lose yourself in the service of others'.

Words of Wisdom

Words of wisdom are rarely and originally spoken by living persons today which is why this compilation is dedicated to the Dalai Lama and his wisdom. These words offer peace of mind, happiness and contentment. The Dalai Lama (meaning ocean of wisdom) is the head of Tibetan Buddhism

A to Zen of Life

A Avoid negative sources, people, places and habits.
B Believe in yourself
C Consider things from every angle.
D Don't give up, and don't give in.
E Everything you are looking for lies behind the mask you wear.
F Family and friends are hidden treasure, seek them and enjoy them.
G Give more than you planned to.
H Hang on to your dreams.
I If opportunity doesn't knock then build a door.
J Judge your success by what you had to give up in order to get it.
K Keep trying no matter how hard it seems.
L Love yourself.
M Make it happen.
N Never lie, steal or cheat.
O Open your arms to change, but never let go of values.
P Practice makes perfect.
Q Quality not quantity in anything you do.
R Remember that silence is sometimes the best answer.
S Stop procrastinating, and instead respond with efficiency.
T Take control of your own destiny.
U Understand yourself in order to better understand others.
V Visualise it.
W When you lose, don't lose the lesson.
X Xcellence in all your efforts.
Y You are unique, nothing can replace you.
Z Zero in on your target and go for it.

* * * * * *

A touch of humour for all those faced with their tax returns

* * * * * *

British Tax Return – This example shows the
importance of accuracy in your tax return.
HMRC (Her Majesty's Revenue & Customs) has returned
the Tax Return to a man in Cleobury Mortimer after he
apparently answered one of the questions incorrectly.

In response to the question:
'Do you have anyone dependent on you?'
he wrote:
2.1 million illegal immigrants.
1.1 million crack-heads.
4.4 million unemployable Jeremy Kyle scroungers.
900,000 criminals in over 85 prisons.
650 idiots in Parliament.
The whole of the European Commission.
Response:
HMRC stated that the response was 'unacceptable'.
Further response:
The man's response back to HMRC was
'Sorry, who did I miss out?

* * * * * *

TWENTY THREE

The Two Ronnies four candles / fork handles sketch

This script was penned by Ronnie Barker in the 1970's and it went on to be voted one of the greatest TV sketches. The sketch features Ronnie Corbett as a shopkeeper who becomes irritated by workman Ronnie Barker, as the customer with his requests for items with double-meanings. It includes the classic opener where Corbett produces four candles when Barker insists he actually wanted fork handles.

It features an old fashioned ironmonger's shop; a bit like Mumfords, a shop that sells everything – garden equipment, ladies tights, builders supplies, mousetraps, everything. The shop has a long counter up and down, a door to the left, lots of deep drawers, and cupboards up high, so that little Ronnie has to get a ladder to get some of the goods that Ronnie Barker orders.

The main actors are Ronnie Corbett and Ronnie Barker who play shopkeeper and customer.
The shopkeeper (Ronnie Corbett) is behind the counter, wearing a warehouse jacket and hat. He has just finished serving a customer.

Shopkeeper (muttering) There you are. Mind how you go.

(Customer enters the shop, wearing a scruffy tank top and beanie).

<u>Customer</u> - Fork 'andles
Shopkeeper - Four candles
<u>Customer</u> - Fork 'andles

(The shop keeper makes for a box, and gets out four candles. He places them on the counter).

Customer - No, fork 'andles.
Shopkeeper (confused) - Well there you are, four candles!
Customer - No, fork 'andles! 'andles for forks!

(The shopkeeper puts the candles away, and goes to get a pitchfork handle. He places it on to the counter)

Shopkeeper - (muttering) Fork 'andles. Thought you said four candles.
Customer - Got any plugs?
Shopkeeper - Plugs. What kind of plugs?
Customer - Rubber one, bathroom.
(The shopkeeper gets out a box of bath plugs, and places it on the counter)
Shopkeeper - (pulling out two different sized plugs) What size?
Customer - Thirteen amp.
Shopkeeper - (muttering) It's electric bathroom plugs, we call them, in the trade. Electric bathroom plugs. (he puts the box away, gets out another box, and places on the counter an electric plug, then puts the box away)
Customer - Saw tips
Shopkeeper - Sore tips? (pause) What d' you want? Ointment, or something like that?
Customer - No, saw tips for covering saws
Shopkeeper - Oh, haven't got any, haven't got any (he mutters) Comin' in, but we haven' got any.
Customer - Got any O's
Shopkeeper - O's
Customer - O's
Shopkeeper - (He gets a garden hoe, and places it on the counter)
Custopmer - No, O's!
Shopkeeper - 'Ose! I thought you said 'oe's (he takes the hoe back, and gets a hose, whilst muttering) When you said 'O's, I thought you said 'Ose! (He places the hose on to the counter)
Customer - No, O's!

Shopkeeper - (confused for a moment) O's? Oh you mean panty 'ose. Panty 'ose! (he picks up a pair of tights from beside him)

Customer - No, no O's for the gate. Mon repose! O's! Letter O's!

Shopkeeper - (finally realising) Letter O's (muttering) You had me going there!

(He climbs up a stepladder, gets a box down, puts the ladder away, and takes the box to the counter, and searches thorough it for letter O)

Shopkeeper - How many d' ya want?

Customer - Two

(The shopkeeper leaves two letter O's on the counter, gets out the ladder, puts the box away, then puts the ladder away, then returns to the counter)

Shopkeeper - Yes, next?

Customer - Got any Ps?

Shopkeeper - (annoyed) For Gawds' sake, why didn' you bleedin' tell me that while I was up there? I'm up and down the shop already, it's up and down the bleedin' shop all the time. (He gets the ladder out again, climbs up and gets the box of letters down again, then puts the ladder away) Honestly. I've got all this shop, I ain't got any help, it's worth it we plan things. How many do y want? (He puts the box on the counter, and gets out some letter P's. How many d'you want? Two?

Customer - No! Tins of peas. Three tins of peas.

Shopkeeper - You're 'avin me on, ain't yer?,yer 'avin' me on?

Customer - No I ain't. I meant tinned peas.

(The shopkeeper dumps the box under the counter, and gets three tins of peas).

Shopkeeper - (placing the tins on the counter) Here we are, right.

Customer - Got any pumps?

Shopkeeper - Pumps? 'and pumps or foot pumps?

Customer - (surprised he has to ask) Foot pumps.

Shopkeeper - (muttering as he goes down the shop) Foot pumps. See a foot pump? (He sees one and picks it up) Tidy up in 'ere. (He puts the pump down on the counter)

Customer - No, pumps for ya feet! Brown pumps, size nine!

Shopkeeper - (almost at breaking point) You are 'avin me on, you are definitely 'avin' me on!

Customer - (not taking much notice of Corbett's mood) I'm not!

Shopkeeper - You are 'avin' me on, (He takes back the pump, gets a pair of brown foot pumps out of a drawer in a temper and slams them on the counter)

Customer - Washers!

Shopkeeper - (extremely close to breaking point) What, dishwashers, floor washers, car washers, windscreen washers, back scrubbers, lavatory cleaners?

Customer - 'Alf inch washers!

Shopkeeper - Oh tap-washers, tap washers! (He very nearly breaks, and snatches the customers list) Look, I've had just about enough of this, give us that list. (he mutters) I'll get it all myself! What's this! (Reading through the list) What's this? (finally breaks) Oh that does it! That just about does it! I have just about had enough of this! (calling through to the back) Mr. Jones! You come out and serve this customer please. I have just about had enough of 'im, (Mr Jones comes out, and the shopkeeper shows him the list). Look what 'e's got on there! Look what 'e's got on there!

Mr Jones (who goes to a drawer with a towel hanging out of it, and opens it) Right! How many would ya like? One or two?

(He moves the towel to reveal the label on the drawer – 'Bill hooks', the joke most likely being the shopkeeper misreading the customer's handwriting as 'bollocks' or 'pillocks')

TWENTY FOUR

A generation ago, schools fostered harmonious
relationships between children, their parents and others.
All children were taught Good Manners and
The Golden Rule as the basis of their interaction with others.
This poster for GOOD MANNERS was produced in 1889 –

* * * * *

GOOD MANNERS

Based upon Rules of the
Children's National Guild of Courtesy

Courtesy, Politeness, or Good Manners, means kindly and thoughtful consideration for others. A celebrated writer has said that a boy who is Courteous and Pure is an honour to his Country. Brave and Noble men and women are always courteous. Three of the bravest and greatest men who ever lived – The Duke of Wellington, General Gordon and General Washington – were distinguished by their courteous behaviour.

Courteous boys and girls will always be careful
to observe the following RULES.

TO THEMSELVES   Be honest, truthful and pure.
Do not use bad language. Keep out of bad company. Keep your face and hands clean, and your clothes and boots, brushed and neat.

AT HOME   Help your parents as much as you can, and do your best to please them.
Be kind to your brothers and sisters.
Do not be selfish, but share all your good things.

AT SCHOOL   Be respectful to your teachers, and help them as much as you can; their work is very difficult and trying. Observe the School rules. Do not 'copy' nor cheat in any way. Never let another be punished in mistake for yourself, this is cowardly and mean.

AT PLAY   Do not cheat at games. Do not bully, only cowards do this. Be pleasant and not quarrelsome. Do not jeer at your schoolmates, or call them by names which they do not like.

IN THE STREET   Salute all your Ministers, teachers and acquaintances when you meet them; they will salute you in return. Do not push nor run against people. Do not chalk on doors, walls nor gates. Do not throw stones nor destroy property. Do not make slides on the pavement, nor throw orange peel or banana skins there; dangerous accidents often result from these practices. Do not make fun of old or crippled people, but be particularly polite to them, as well as to strangers and foreigners.

AT TABLE   Always wash your hands and face before coming to the table. Do not put your knife to your mouth. Look after other people, do not help yourself only. Do not be greedy. Do not speak with food or drink in your mouth. Turn your head away from the table and put your hand or handkerchief before your mouth when you sneeze or cough. Do not sit with your elbows on the table.

EVERYWHERE   Never be rude to anyone, whether older or younger, whether richer or poorer, than yourself. Remember to say 'Please' or 'Thank you' 'Yes sir' or 'Yes ma'am' or 'No sir' or 'No ma'am'. Before entering a room it is often courteous to knock at the door. Do not forget to close the door quietly after you. Always show attention to older people and strangers by opening the door for them, bringing what they require (hat, chair, etc.) giving up your seat to them if necessary, and in every possible way saving them trouble. Never interrupt when a person is speaking. Always mind your own business. Be punctual. Be tidy.

REMEMBER THE
GOLDEN RULE   All these rules respecting your conduct towards others are included in the one 'GOLDEN RULE 'Always do to others as you would wish them to do to you if you were in their place'. Whenever, therefore, you are in doubt as to how you should act towards others, ask yourself this question, 'How should I like them to act towards me if I were in their place?' and then - Do what your conscience tells you is right.

These rules covered personal conduct at home, at school and in the street.

The chart was hung in a prominent place in the classroom, and as part of the lessons on 'conduct and manners', the teacher would run through the chart, while the children repeated each rule. The students were then required to then put into practice, in the classroom and playground, the instruction received.

Simples!

The end.